Say It with Stitches

D1604904

love

b

Mom

Bling

sweet
dreams

PINK
tickled

B

Say It with Stitches

New Embroidery Designs for Letters and Words

SHARON AND KRISTIN JANKOWICZ

Creative Publishing international

Chanhassen, MN

Sharon and Kristin Jankowicz, mother and daughter, design projects for the craft industry. Each a professional graphic designer and versatile needle-crafter, they are a witty, dynamic design duo. Their collaborative fine art, mixed media, altered art pieces, needlework, and craft pieces are sold to private collectors as well as the craft industry, editors, publishers, and manufacturers. Sharon has taught calligraphy to hundreds of students and has worked as a professional calligrapher for over 25 years. That amounts to hand lettering literally thousands of wedding invitations! Kristin majored in graphic design, with a special interest in typography, at both the University of Illinois and at Central St. Martin's College of Art & Design in London, England. Every project created in their Illinois studio has the fingerprints of both all over it.

Creative Publishing international

Copyright 2007
Creative Publishing international
18705 Lake Drive East
Chanhassen, Minnesota 55317
1-800-328-3895
www.creativepub.com
All rights reserved

President/CEO: Ken Fund

Executive Editor: Alison Brown Cerier
Managing Editor: Barbara Harold
Senior Editor: Linda Neubauer
Photo Stylist: Joanne Wawra
Creative Director: Brad Springer
Photo Art Director: Tim Himsel
Photographer: Steve Galvin, Andrea Rugg, Joel Schnell
Production Manager: Linda Halls
Cover Design: Brian Donahue, BE Design, Inc.
Page Design and Layout: Peter M. Blaiwas, Vern Associates, Inc.

Library of Congress Cataloging-in-Publication Data

Jankowicz, Sharon.
  Say it with stitches : new embroidery designs for letters and words /
Sharon Jankowicz, Kristin Jankowicz.
     p. cm.
ISBN-13: 978-1-58923-270-9 (hardcover)
  ISBN-10: 1-58923-270-4 (hardcover)
  1. Embroidery. I. Jankowicz, Kristin. II. Title.
TT770.J36 2007
  746.44--dc22   2006017603

Printed in Singapore
10 9 8 7 6 5 4 3 2

Contents

Say It Your Way   6

The Letters   7

The Projects   12
Thinking Cap   12
Bravo Label   16
Baseball Tee   20
Love Card   24
Sweet Dreams Lullaby Linens   28
Personalized Pillowcase   32
Spit Happens Burp Cloth   34
Aloha Tee   38
XOX Tee   42
Rock Me Jean Jacket   44
Super Initial Jeans   46
Monogram Cuff   48
I Do! Keepsake Ribbon   50
Crewel Monogram Pillow   52
Bling Tank   54
Mom Christmas Stocking   58
Girls Tee   60
Tickled Pink Onesie   64
Say Cheese Camera Tag   68
Smile Tag   70

It's EZ When You Know How   72
Get Ready   72
Get Set   83
Stitch   88
Get Creative   102

The Alphabet Patterns   105
Typewriter Type-ography   105
Happy Cursive Handwriting   106
Bubble Graffiti A-Zs   107
Elegant Classic Calligraphy   108
Urban Gothic Text   110

Sources   111

Acknowledgments and Dedication   112

Say It Your Way

What's on your mind? *Say It With Stitches* is here to help you express yourself with hand-stitched letters, words, and phrases.

Do you think you're too busy to enjoy crafting? Embroidery is the ideal craft for people with hectic schedules who need some soothing down time. This is a book full of fun, contemporary stitching and cross-craft projects that you can finish in a day or less. Plus, embroidery is portable; just pop it in a bag and take it along with you.

All of these projects use free-form embroidery, so there are no painstaking, confusing charts or tedious counting. At the back of the book is a how-to section, with all the basics for you beginners, and new perspectives and challenges to keep you experienced embroiderers in stitches.

We'll show you how to create upscale, fashionista looks without breaking the bank. Buy off the rack and embellish. You'll save money—embroidery materials are surprisingly inexpensive—while satisfying your passion for posh and unique fashion.

You're the designer, and you have oodles of options for making each project your very own.

LETTERING STYLES–You choose the alphabet style. We've made embroidery patterns for five very different, but all very hip, alphabets for spelling out your own words: Typewriter Type-ography, Bubble Graffiti A–Zs, Urban Gothic Text, Happy Cursive Handwriting, and Elegant Classic Calligraphy.

WORDS–To prime your eloquence, we've come up with an array of 20 trendy to classic (but never stodgy) letter, word, or phrase patterns for you to stitch. Each is shown as part of a step-by-step project. We've brainstormed some alternative words for your projects, too; you'll find them under the heading "more ideas." We're sure that after you read through some of our ideas, you'll be ready to make a statement of your own.

PROJECTS–You can "spread the word" on jeans, tees, ball caps, gift containers, your cell phone, tags, cards, scrapbooks, ribbons, bed linens, wedding items, and baby things. How about embroidery on vintage clothing, belts, purses, underwear, or towels? The step-by-step projects share methods and tips for embroidering on all kinds of objects.

THREADS–Select from a zillion colors of embroidery floss, sparkling metallic thread, sheer opalescent thread, super-easy-to-use pearl cotton, sumptuous silk thread, dimensional crewel wool, novelty yarns, trendy trims, or even braiding. There's more about threads in the basics section.

STITCHES–Use your favorite embroidery stitches. For newbies and those of you who need a little technique brush up or want to add to your repertoire, there are easy-to-follow instructions and step-by-step illustrations for basic embroidery stitches.

TECHNIQUES–Choose a cross-craft technique to accent your project—appliqué, reverse appliqué, crewel embroidery, paper-craft, painting, and of course beading! The "It's EZ When You Know How" (page 72) section has the instructions and information about materials and techniques that will help you to get stellar results. Throughout the book, we've scattered tips that are either standard stitching wisdom or our voice of experience speaking to you.

Read all about our alphabets, explore the projects, check out the techniques, then get your stitch on!

–Sharon and Kristin

The Letters

We've designed some prime lettering styles for you to embroider, so your projects will be right on trend. All of these alphabets have roots in established letterforms, but these letters are interpreted with our own personal twist. We've styled them all to be "embroider-able."

Letters are an art form. Just like the notes in music, movements in dance, and strokes and colors in painting, letterforms are expressive. Each alphabet has a distinct personality and connotations. Here are some word associations to give you some ideas of what we think each alphabet communicates. No doubt you'll have some of your own impressions! You'll want to match the feeling emanating from the letterform to the message that you want your words to express.

Typewriter Type-ography

inspired by the serif fonts found on old-fashioned manual typewriters

Trendy Familiar Functional Practical
Eclectic Vintage Contemporary Versatile

This is a vintage machine-made font with contemporary appeal. The typeface is enjoying new popularity with artists in many areas because it meshes well with other styles. Kind of like tofu, it becomes infused with the flavor of whatever it is mixed with. This font will work well on everything from heirloom scrapbook page titles to kids' clothes.

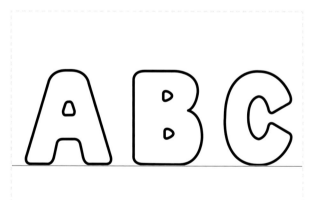

Bubble Graffiti A-Zs

inspired by spontaneously drawn, freehand graffiti lettering

Hip Contemporary Playful Whimsical
Quirky Cartoonish Animated Fun Funky
Sassy Cheeky

This alphabet is named Bubble Graffiti because its large open shape allows you to overlap the letters in words like graffiti often does. You can overlap a small portion of each letter onto the letter right next to it. Also like graffiti, the letters don't even have to be in a straight line. We choose this style when we're trying to be witty. It's also great for kid projects—baby to teen.

Happy Cursive Hand

inspired by free, quick, everyday handwriting

- -

Fresh Soft Personal Warm Comfy Casual
Easy Breezy Conversational Pretty Retro
Perky Playful Fanciful Whimsical Cheery Sweet

Use Happy Cursive Hand when you're in a peachy mood. It's nice for greeting cards and projects when you want to make someone smile. If you're in a hurry, a plus is that it stitches up in a flash.

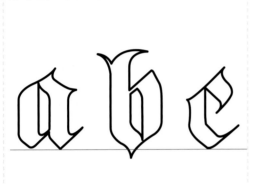

Urban Gothic Text

inspired by Old English, Blackletter, and Gothic book text

- -

Edgy Dramatic Sexy Bold Solid Stately Spiritual
Religious Historic Architectural Chic Ultramodern

Gothic text is lettered with a flat, broad-nib pen. The thick parts, the downstrokes, are formed by pulling the nib straight down, while the thin parts are made by moving the nib sideways. Historically used for hand lettering religious text, nowadays you'll see everything from Christmas card lettering to vampire movie titles and tattoo flash—ironic!

This lettering is a "Goth" style staple and a signature of Generation Y. It speaks to today's designers because of its intriguing sense of history merged with today's urban culture. Artistically, it's a fascinating juxtaposition of angular and flowing forms and lines. It's a visually interesting graphic ornament like paisley or a fleur de lis.

Gothic lettering is an extremely popular trend, but it can be really hard to read, almost illegible. And that's perfectly OK, because right now that's straight up style. Its esthetic and associations are what the designer wants you to realize. If you can actually read the words, that's just a bonus! If you do intend for your Gothic letters to be read, stitch the outline, and then fill in the letters with fabric paint or satin stitches.

Elegant Classic Calligraphy

inspired by English Roundhand, Edwardian, Copperplate, and Spencerian formal penmanship

- -

Delicate Romantic Exquisite Light Graceful
Sophisticated Traditional Formal Proper
High-end Extravagant Classic

This script is formed by a pen that has a very flexible, pointed steel nib. The downstrokes of the letter are made by using pressure, and the fine, hairline strokes are made by releasing the pressure and barely skimming the nib across the paper. This calligraphic style continues to be the hands-down, time-honored, favorite style of lettering for wedding invitations and monograms.

How to Use the Alphabets

Most of the projects in this book include a fab word or letter pattern all ready for you to embroider. The patterns are provided at the same size used in the project. But we know there are times when you'll want to use an alternate thought from the "more ideas" lists or you'll have some of your own ideas. Here's how to make your own pattern—it's easy as A B C!

COPY THE LETTERS– Decide which style has the right flavor for your project. Then use a copy machine to reproduce the letters you need, reducing or enlarging them to the perfect size. Cut out the letters, carefully trimming close to the outlines of the letter patterns.

DESIGN THE LAYOUT– Draw a baseline for your layout on white cardstock or paper. Most times you'll use a ruler to draw a straight line. You can use a compass or trace the shape of something round or oval to draft an arc. Experiment with other layouts as well.

Arrange your cut-out letters on the white cardstock. The alphabet patterns have a baseline to help you keep your lettering in a straight line and at a uniform slant. Align the baselines as a guide to line up your letters. You don't stitch the baseline. Aim to keep the spacing between the letters even looking. Sometimes the connecting strokes between letters might need to be adjusted so they look right for your design. Use an ordinary pencil to draw any changes to the letters. When you decide on the placement of the letters, tape the individual letters in place on the cardstock.

MAKE THE PATTERN– Use a copy machine to make a copy of the final layout, or tape a fresh piece of tracing paper over your whole layout, and then trace over your design with a fine tip permanent marker. You've created your own personalized pattern. Now just transfer the pattern onto your fabric and get stitching!

INITIAL CAPS–Some alphabets have only lower case (small) letters or only upper case (capital) letters. When you're using one of these alphabets and you'd ordinarily use a capital letter to start a name or word, use an "initial cap." Just make the initial letter a little bit larger than the other letters.

CENTERING–The center of your design is not necessarily the middle of the middle letter. To find the center of your design, just fold the pattern in half, matching the beginning of the first word to the end of the last word. Mark the center fold with a transfer pen or pencil. Then simply match the center of your pattern to the spot on your fabric where you want the center of the embroidered design to be.

INITIALS AND MONOGRAMS–An initial is just the first letter of a name. Embroider either a given (first) or surname (last) initial or the three initials of the given name, middle name, and surname in that order. Each letter is the same size and can be arranged in a straight line from top to bottom, left to right, or in a descending diagonal line from left to right.

A monogram is a unique design or emblem consisting of initials that represent one person, a couple, or a family. A monogram is an exclusive symbol, like a logo. That's why a custom designed, hand-stitched monogram is the epitome of a very thoughtful and impressive gift.

The letters of a monogram for one person can be arranged on a flat baseline. The surname initial is the largest letter, positioned in the center. The given name initial and the middle name initials should be the same size, smaller than the surname initial; the given name initial is on the left side and the middle name initial is on the right side. The monogram for Patricia Renee Morris would look like this:

The letters of a monogram for a husband and wife can be arranged on a flat baseline or with the larger surname initial reaching lower and higher than the other initials. The wife's given name initial is on the left side and the husband's given name initial is on the right. The monogram for Olivia and Robert Millington would look like this:

To draft a monogram, begin by making reduced or enlarged copies of the letters you need. If you want to overlap letters, trace your copied letters onto tracing paper, so you can see all of the parts of each letter. Cut out the letters, carefully trimming close to the outlines of the letter patterns. Mark the lines for your layout on white cardstock. Align the cut-out letters on your baseline. Play with the placement of your cut-out letters, layering them on top of each other to overlap parts of them if you like. When you decide on your arrangement, tape the individual letters in place.

If you're in the mood to show off your artistic flair, add some swashes and flourishes. Draw your own or trace them from these monogram samples. Experiment with their placement to discover how they can enhance your monogram design. When you find an arrangement that you like, tape it in place. Erase or white-out any lines that you don't want in your pattern.

At this point you can use a copy machine to make a copy of the layout or tape a fresh piece of tracing paper over your whole layout, and then trace the final monogram design with a fine tip permanent marker. This is your customized pattern. Transfer the pattern to your project, and embroider your one-of-a-kind creation!

Here are a few more examples of how initials are traditionally arranged in a three-letter monogram. Copy the swash and flourish elements of these monograms to help you design your monogram, or add your own special flourishes.

Thinking

Next time you need to put on your thinking cap, you'll have one. This is a clever gift for a college kid cramming for exams or a close friend making a major life decision. The instructions demo the best way to transfer a pattern onto a curved surface like this cap. It's even easier to stitch words on a visor with a soft band.

1 Trace the letters onto tracing paper with an ordinary lead pencil. Enlarge or reduce the word to the desired size with a copy machine.

2 Trace the word again onto tracing paper, making any adjustments in the letter placement/spacing on the tracing paper.

3 Trace the design onto transfer mesh, using a transfer pen.

4 Fold the transfer mesh in half, matching the beginning of the first letter to the end of the last letter. Mark the center.

You'll need...

Cap or visor

Tracing paper

Pencil

Transfer material

Straight pins

Transfer marker

Chenille needle, size 22

Cotton pearl thread, size 5: very dark royal blue

Tapestry needle, size 22

Craft shears

Thread conditioner

Needle puller

Thimble

Embroidery scissors

More ideas...

head case

bad hair day

gear head

remember

5 Place the center mark over the center of the cap. Pin the transfer mesh to the cap.

6 Trace over the pattern with a transfer marker, to mark the design on the cap.

7 Thread the chenille needle with dark blue pearl thread. *Backstitch* the letters.

8 Thread the tapestry needle with dark blue pearl thread. Do the whipping step of the *whipped backstitch* over the letters.

thinking

Tips on transfer materials

Transfer materials (page 80) conform to the shape of your project. Stitch Witchery (fusible adhesive without paper backing) works very well as a transfer material.

Patterns drawn on transfer material with permanent marker can be saved and reused. Save your pattern in an envelope marked with the word and style of lettering so that you can use it again for other projects or share it with a friend.

Transfer material is reusable when you trace the design the first time with an erasable fabric marker. Simply rinse it with water.

Bravo

You can turn a plain container into a gift by covering it with an artsy label and trims. We used a shiny, new paint can from the paint store. You can choose from many interesting containers at the craft store, or think green and recycle something. Fill the container with goodies for a double gift.

1 To determine the size of your label, measure the height and circumference of your container and add ½" (1.3 cm) to the circumference to overlap the edges in the back. Mark these dimensions on the fabric.

2 Trace the letters onto tracing paper with an ordinary lead pencil. Enlarge or reduce the word to the desired size with a copy machine.

3 Trace the word again onto tracing paper, making any adjustments in the letter placement/spacing on the tracing paper. Transfer the lettering design onto your label.

4 Cut the fabric far enough beyond the label outline to fit the letters in an embroidery hoop. Put the fabric in a hoop.

You'll need...

Clean container

Fabric to cover the sides of your container

Tools/materials for transferring the design

Embroidery hoop

Chenille needle, size 22

Cotton pearl thread, size 5, in contrasting color

Tapestry needle, size 22

Embroidery scissors

Tape

Jewel glue

Ribbon

Trims

17

More ideas...

Congrats!

Happy Birthday!

Trick or Treat!

Enjoy!

5 Thread the chenille needle with pearl thread and *backstitch* the letters.

6 Thread the tapestry needle with pearl thread and work the whipping step of *whipped backstitches*.

7 Remove the embroidery hoop. Trim the fabric to the marked shape.

8 Adhere the label to your container with a thin, even coat of jewel glue.

9 Glue on ribbon, trim, buttons, charms, or whatever strikes your fancy.

World of Thanks... add these words to your embroidery repertoire!

merci (French)

gracias (Spanish)

grazie (Italian)

arigato (Japanese)

danke schön (German)

mahalo (Hawaiian)

ahsante (Swahili)

dziekuje (Polish)

taka bra (Swedish)

takk (Norwegian)

koszonom (Hungarian)

gratiam (Latin)

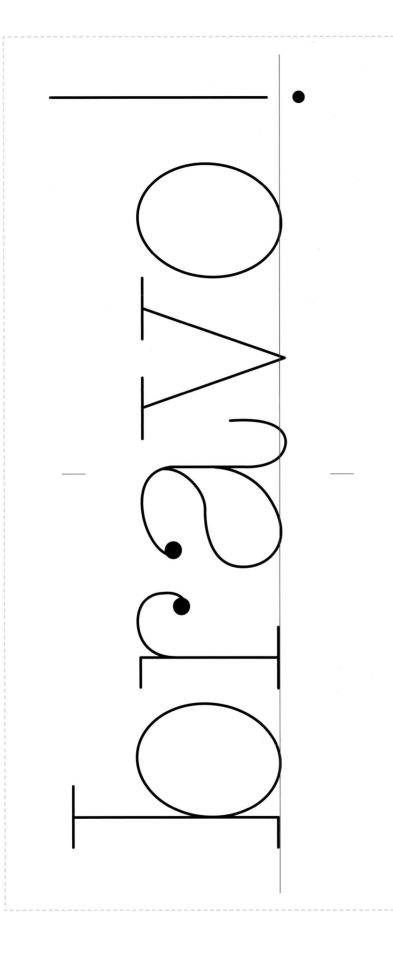

Tips for stitching labels

Felt is the ideal fabric for a quick label project because its cut edges won't fray. It's trendy to boot.

If you choose a **thin or knit fabric** for your label, bond it to a lightweight, iron-on interfacing or fabric stabilizer. Use a thread conditioner to help your needle and thread move smoothly through the interfacing.

Don't use knots in your thread when you're stitching a label or flat project like a tag or card; they pop up and make bumps on the front when you glue down the label. Tape down the tails instead.

Baseball

B is for baseball! A felt appliqué baseball on this sporty tee adds dimension, while the baseball lacing borders bring the whole baseball motif home. Change the B to the sport fan's initial, if you wish. To save time you could skip the felt appliqué steps and just stitch the whole pattern onto a shirt. Baseball PJs are a big hit—be sure to add the baseball lacing border to the leg hems.

You'll need...

T-shirt

Iron and ironing board

Tools/materials for transferring the design

Chenille needle, size 22

Cotton pearl thread, size 5: red, tangerine, and lemon

Paper-backed fusible adhesive sheet

Felted wool, white

Fabric shears

Embroidery scissors

Embroidery hoop

1   Wash and iron your fabric.

2   Use a transfer pen or pencil to mark the location of center line and two side rows of the baseball lacing border around each sleeve opening.

3   To imitate baseball lacing, stitch this border: *Backstitch* the center line in red pearl thread (or light gray for a more realistic

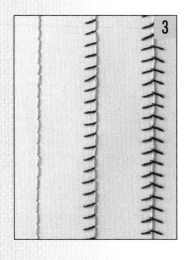

Tips on borders

Use the seams and their stitching as a **guide** for border trimming embroidery. If you're a perfectionist, you can count the existing stitches in the seams to very accurately space the distance between your embellishing stitches. However, a bit of imperfection adds charm.

effect). Use red pearl thread to *straight stitch* a row of short diagonal lines first down one side and then the other.

4 Transfer the circle outline for the ball onto the paper backing of the fusible web. Fuse the adhesive to the back of the felt, following the manufacturer's directions. Cut out the ball, using fabric shears. Remove the paper backing. Fuse the ball to your tee.

5 Copy and transfer the baseball pattern onto your fabric. Enlarge the letter that you've selected to about 2½" (6.5 cm) tall, and transfer it to the center of the ball. (Be sure to fuse the circle to the tee before transferring the pattern. Ironing can permanently set some transfer marks, so don't take that chance.)

6 Put the fabric in an embroidery hoop, centering the ball and taking care not to stretch the fabric.

7 Stitch the baseball lacing onto the ball using red pearl thread.

8 *Running stitch* a circle near the edge of the ball, using lemon pearl thread.

9 *Chain stitch* the letter, using tangerine pearl thread.

10 Outline the letter with *split stitches*, using lemon pearl thread.

11 *Backstitch* around the edge of the baseball, on the tee, using tangerine pearl thread.

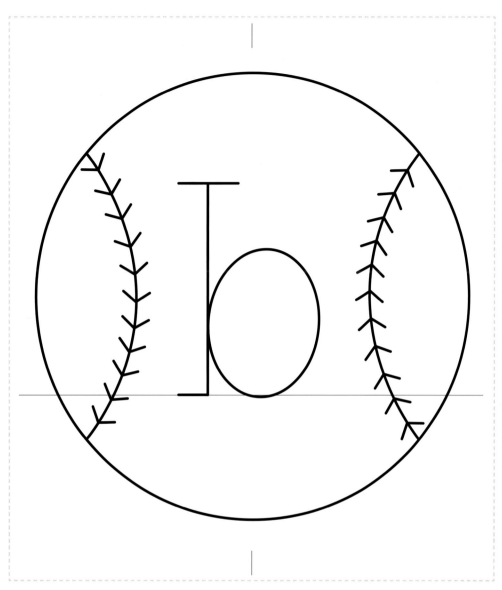

Love

Card makers are discovering how wonderful stitching looks on paper! Set the mood with paper colors and patterns—from perky to soothing. The size of the card you make can be determined by the length of the wording and sometimes by the size of envelope that you'll use for mailing the card. You can stitch on bookmarks and tags, too.

1 Trim the paper and cardstock to the sizes you desire. Fold the plain pumpkin cardstock in half to form the card.

2 Enlarge or reduce the desired letters, and trace them onto tracing paper, joining them in cursive writing and making any adjustments in the letter placement/spacing on the tracing paper. Transfer the word pattern onto the striped cardstock.

3 Mark dots on the letter lines where you want the stitches to be, about $\frac{1}{8}$" (3 mm) apart.

You'll need...

Pumpkin solid cardstock

Pumpkin striped cardstock

Pale lavender dotted paper

Craft scissors

Tools/materials for transferring the design

Self-healing cutting mat

Mouse pad

Paper piercer

Tapestry needle

Cotton pearl thread, size 5: lemon and plum

Double-sided tape

Embroidery scissors

Beading needle

Cotton embroidery floss: plum

Glass beads, assorted

More ideas...

¿qué pasa?

c'est la vie

ooh la la!

fiddle dee dee

luck

thanks

4 Place the cutting mat on your work surface. Put the mouse pad facedown on the cutting mat. Using a paper piercer, poke holes at the marked dots.

5 Thread the tapestry needle with plum pearl thread. *Double running stitch* the letters. Instead of knotting the thread at the beginning and end, tape the thread tails to the back of the cardstock.

6 Adhere the stitched striped cardstock to the center of the dot paper with double-sided tape. Adhere the dot paper to the card front with double-sided tape.

7 Mark dots where you want the cross-stitch pattern to be. Pierce the dots as in step 4.

8 Embroider diagonal *straight stitches* in one direction, then reverse and work diagonal *straight stitches* in the opposite direction to create the cross-stitch pattern.

9 Thread the beading needle with a single strand of plum embroidery floss. Run the needle through several glass beads, ending with a seed bead, then going back up through the other beads.

10 Hang the beads from one of the cross-stitches with a tiny embroidery floss bow. Stitch through the cardstock to secure the bow.

Tips for stitching on paper

Read **"Stitch on Paper and Cardstock"** (page 103) for need-to-know info.

Running stitches are great for papercrafting because the back is relatively smooth and will lie flat.

A **double running stitch** forms a more legible letter than a running stitch.

Sweet Dreams

Express your affection for an overnight guest by leaving a delightful bedtime message on the pillow in the guest room. This decorative pillowcase is embroidered with subdued pastel colors and sprinkled with twinkling crystal stars, sparkling seed beads, and a delicate ivory crescent moon—the things that sweet dreams are made of! Check out the tips for embroidering on bed linens on page 73.

1 Wash and iron the fabric.

2 Copy the pattern and transfer it onto the fabric. Put your fabric in the embroidery hoop.

3 *Couch* the word "sweet," using six strands of the multicolored floss as the laid thread and a single strand of beading thread as the couching thread.

4 Secure a rose petite bead at each couching stitch, using a single strand of beading thread and a beading needle.

You'll need...

Pillowcase

Tools/materials for transferring the design

Embroidery hoop large enough to fit the entire design

Crewel needles, size 3 and 10

Cotton embroidery floss: variegated pink, ecru, and very light pink

Clear beading thread

Antique rose petite beads

Bcading needle

Tapestry needle, size 26

Embroidery scissors

Ultraluscent seed beads

Jewel glue

More ideas...

good night

sleep tight

bless you

dream

shhhh

Tips for choosing threads

Overdyed silk thread is luxurious, but it is also delicate and must be hand washed or dry cleaned.

Cotton floss is sturdier, color-fast, and can be machine washed.

There are lots of gorgeous yarns and trims that would look great as a **couched thread.** Just be sure to match the care needs of your thread to the care needs of the fabric you're couching it onto.

5 *Running stitch* the word "dreams" with two strands of ecru embroidery floss. Thread the tapestry needle with two strands of light pink embroidery floss, and work the weaving step of the *woven running stitch* following the illustration for woven back-stitch on page 99.

6 Remove the embroidery hoop. Attach the stars, moon, and beads with a beading needle and one strand of clear beading thread or thread that matches your fabric. If your stars or moon don't have holes for sewing, adhere them with jewel glue, and let the glue dry completely.

7 Turn the pillowcase inside out and apply a small drop of jewel glue onto each knot and thread tail on the back of your embroidery.

sweet

dreams

Personalized

Kids love to embroider, too. Here's a fun activity for a slumber party. Transfer each girl's name on the hem of a pillowcase before the party. Then teach them these easy stitches. They'll be delighted with the cool weaving effects.

You'll need...

Pillowcase

Craft shears

Transfer paper

Ballpoint pen

Chenille needle, size 22

Cotton pearl thread, size 5: light yellow, cranberry

Tapestry needle, size 22

Embroidery scissors

Clear beading thread

Beading needle

1 Wash and iron the fabric.

2 Enlarge the letters that you want to use. Cut them out, trimming close to the outlines. Arrange the letters on a sheet of paper, and tape them in place.

3 Position transfer paper on the pillowcase, and tape it in place. Place the sheet of lettering on top of the transfer paper, and tape it in place. Transfer the design to the pillowcase by tracing the outlines of the letters with a ballpoint pen. Check to see that the letters have been completely transferred before removing the papers.

4 Put the fabric in a hoop.

5 Thread the chenille needle with light yellow pearl thread. *Backstitch* all of the letters.

6 Thread the tapestry needle with cranberry pearl thread, and weave it through every other stitch creating a *woven backstitch*.

7 Start a new thread, and weave the stitches from the opposite side, creating a *double woven backstitch*.

8 Remove the fabric from the hoop.

9 Stitch beads to the letters as accents, using clear beading thread and a beading needle. See the tips for stitching beads on page 102.

More ideas...

good night

sleep tight

sweet dreams

love ya

- - - - -

Attaching Embellishments

Sewing is the best way to attach most embellishments if you want them to hold up to repeated laundering. Here are some other quick and easy options:

Grosgrain ribbon: adhere with iron-on adhesive

Pompoms: adhere with fabric glue

Beads: adhere with jewel glue

Spit Happens

Super soft micro-fiber fleece makes this burp cloth comfy and cushy for a baby. It rinses out easily and dries very quickly (which is a very good thing for a burp cloth). Trim the edges with a quick and easy border and fringe, or blanket-stitch the edges. To make a security blanket, just cut a bigger rectangle and change the words to *cuddle, snuggle up,* or *born lucky.*

1　Cut a 15" (38 cm) square of each fabric, and round the corners. We used regular fabric shears to cut the yellow micro-fiber fleece and pinking shears to cut out the green fleece.

2　Trace the pattern and transfer it onto the yellow top layer of fabric.

3　Put the marked fabric into an embroidery hoop.

4　Thread the crewel needle with three strands of blue/green variegated embroidery floss. *Chainstitch* the letters.

You'll need...

½ yd. (0.5 m) yellow micro-fiber fleece

½ yd. (0.5 m) light green fleece

Fabric shears

Dressmaker's pinking shears

Tools/materials for transferring the design

Embroidery hoop

Crewel embroidery needle

Cotton embroidery floss: variegated blue/green and variegated yellow/green

Chenille needle, size 22

Cotton pearl thread, size 5: delft blue

Tapestry needle, size 22

Embroidery scissors

35

More ideas...

burp

drool

oops

baby's name

5 Remove the embroidery hoop. Mark a border stitching line 1" (2.5 cm) from the edge of the yellow fabric with a transfer pen or pencil.

6 Lay the yellow fabric over the green fabric, and pin them together inside the marked line.

7 Thread the chenille needle with pearl thread and *running stitch* through both layers on the marked line.

8 Thread the tapestry needle with all six strands of yellow/green variegated embroidery floss. Do the whipping step of the *whipped running stitch* to complete the border.

9 To fringe the edges, snip up close to the border through both layers using fabric shears and making the cuts about ¼" (6 mm) apart.

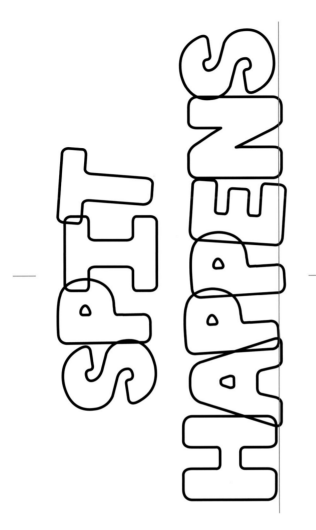

Tips for working with fleece

Pinking shears have a zigzag cutting blade and are intended for fabric. There are papercrafting scissors that have the same style of zigzag blade, but you'll have a hard time getting a clean cut on fleece fabric with them.

Avoid pressing fleece, as this will flatten the pile.

Use **light tension** to keep your stitches from sinking down into this cushy fabric where you won't be able to see them.

Aloha

Bubble letters can easily become appliqués. It's fun to use theme related fabric patterns and trinkets in your designs. This shirt says "Aloha" with a Hawaiian print and flower.

1   Wash and iron the tee and print fabric.

2   Enlarge your letters and print them onto cardstock, leaving some space between them. Cut the letters apart. Then cut out the inside of each letter with a craft knife to create a stencil.

3   Position the stencils over the colors and images on the fabric that you prefer. Tape the stencils in place, then use a transfer pen or pencil to trace the letters.

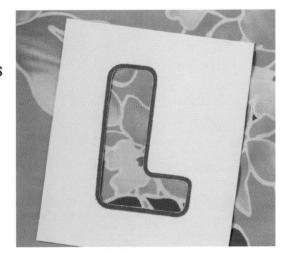

You'll need...

T-shirt

Hawaiian print cotton fabric

Iron and ironing board

Cardstock

Fabric shears

Craft knife

Self-healing cutting mat

Tape

Transfer pen or pencil

Paper-backed fusible adhesive

Chenille needle, size 22

Cotton pcarl thread, size 5: cranberry and light cranberry

Embroidery scissors

Safety pin

Fabric craft flower

More ideas...

channel surfer

your city's name

your team

your school

your club

4   Fuse paper-backed fusible adhesive to the back of the fabric, following the manufacturer's directions. Let the fabric cool, then cut out the letters.

5   Arrange the letters on your tee. Remove the paper backing, and fuse the letters in place.

6   Put your fabric in a hoop.

7   *Couch* around each letter using light cranberry pearl thread as the laid thread and cranberry pearl thread as the couching thread.

8   Outline the couching with *backstitches* of cranberry pearl thread.

9   Remove the hoop. Safety-pin a fabric craft flower on the "O."

Tips for 3-D embellishments

Replace the letter O with a **theme-related object.** Pick something small, light, and somewhat flat, such as a button, large bead, or a charm.

The **dots** over the letters j and i can be replaced with a bead, sequin, or other embellishment, too.

Pin on the embellishment rather than sewing, so you can **remove it** for washing.

XOX

Hugs and kisses! A tee is the quintessential place to say it in stitches—we especially like this front and center area—it's a prime location for a monogram, too. When you stitch on a lightweight or mixed-fiber tee, use a stabilizer (page 82) to support the stitches and prevent the fabric from stretching to the point of breaking stitches.

You'll need...

T-shirt

Tools/materials for transferring the design

Lightweight fusible knit interfacing

Fabric shears

Embroidery hoop

Crewel embroidery needle

Cotton embroidery floss: light blue

Embroidery scissors

Fabric glue

1 Trace the desired letters onto tracing paper. Using a copy machine, enlarge or reduce the word to the desired size.

2 Trace the word again onto tracing paper, making any adjustments in the letter placement/spacing on the tracing paper.

3 Cut a rectangle of fusible interfacing about ½" (1.3 cm) larger all around than your design. Round off the corners of the interfacing. Fuse the interfacing to the wrong side of the tee, following the manufacturer's directions. Allow the fabric to cool.

4 Transfer the design onto your fabric.

5 Put your fabric into an embroidery hoop, taking care not to stretch the fabric.

6 *Running stitch* the lettering with two strands of embroidery floss.

7 Apply a small drop of fabric glue to any knots or loose threads on the back of your embroidery to help keep them secure during laundering.

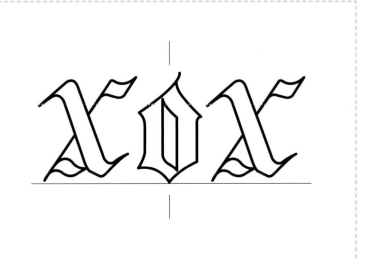

More ideas...

lucky

sweet

chic

bella

wicked

moi?

Rock Me

This design would look righteous on jeans or a tee as well as funky baby clothes. Filling in letters with a permanent metallic marker is a great way to make them easier to read. Use metallic markers and matching metallic floss for a "heavy metal" look. For tips on stitching on denim, see page 73.

You'll need...

Jean jacket

Tools/materials for transferring the design

Embroidery hoop

Metallic floss: copper

Crewel embroidery needle

Embroidery scissors

Permanent marker: metallic copper

1   Wash and iron your fabric.

2   Trace the desired letters onto tracing paper. Using a copy machine, enlarge or reduce the word to the desired size.

3   Trace the word again onto tracing paper, making any adjustments in the letter placement/spacing on the tracing paper.

4   Transfer the design onto your fabric.

5   Put your fabric into an embroidery hoop.

6   *Split stitch* the lettering with two strands of metallic floss.

7   Remove the hoop. Place your fabric over some scrap paper, since markers often bleed through the fabric and stain whatever surface is beneath it. Fill in the letters by coloring with a permanent metallic copper-colored marker. Don't worry about doing a perfect coloring job—you're going for a well-worn look.

More ideas...

rock on

rocker

cry baby

let's roll

Tip for metallic threads

To keep metallic threads from **fraying,** brush the spot where you'll be cutting with jewel glue, let the glue dry completely, then cut with craft scissors. No frayed ends!

Super Initial

Everybody loves one-of-a-kind embellished jeans. Supersize a graphic Gothic letter to swirl around your leg. Add soft color and dimension by cutting away parts of the letter to reveal another fabric underneath (that's called reverse appliqué). We used sturdy felted wool (page 73); any fabric that's about the same weight and strength as denim will work well for backing cut-outs. To learn about stitching on denim and save frustration, check out page 73.

1 Wash and iron your fabric.

2 Enlarge the letter pattern and transfer it onto your fabric.

3 Pin the fabric for the cut-out to the inside of the jeans, making sure the edges extend beyond the design.

4 *Running stitch* the letter with light turquoise pearl thread, stitching through the denim and the felted wool.

5 *Backstitch* an outline of plum pearl thread right next to the running stitching.

6 *Split stitch* another outline of very dark blue violet pearl thread next to the backstitches.

7 Using fabric shears, trim the denim away from the inside of the solid shapes to within ½" (6 mm) of the running stitches. Be very careful not to cut the felted wool.

You'll need...

Jeans

Tools/materials for transferring the design

Safety pins

Felted wool (not craft felt), enough to back your letter, celery green

Chenille needle, size 22

Cotton pearl thread, size 5: light turquoise, plum, very dark blue violet

Needle puller

Thimble

Embroidery scissors

Fabric shears

– – – – –

More ideas...

3 initials stacked

47

Monogram

A monogram on a shirt cuff, pocket, or handkerchief is a touch of sophistication and luxury. When embroidering a dress shirt cuff, position the letter close to the wrist so the distinguished little emblem can be admired even when a jacket is worn over it. If you haven't done much embroidering, begin by stitching a medium-sized monogram on a linen handkerchief or napkin before taking on a more advanced challenge like a small monogram with itsy-bitsy stitches.

You'll need...

Shirt

Wax-free dressmaker's tracing paper

Fine ballpoint pen

Crewel needle, fine

Cotton embroidery floss: white

Tapestry needle, fine

Thread conditioner

Needle puller

Thimble

Embroidery scissors

48

1   Wash and iron your fabric.

2   Trace the desired letter, and reduce it, using a copy machine. Transfer it onto your fabric, using dressmaker's tracing paper and a fine ballpoint pen (see page 80).

3   Thread a fine crewel needle with a single strand of white embroidery floss, and *backstitch* the entire outline of the design.

4   Thread a fine tapestry needle with a single strand of white embroidery floss, and work the whipping step of the *whipped backstitch* over the entire design.

5   *Satin stitch* across the wide downstroke(s) of your letter with two strands of white floss.

6   Use one strand of white floss to whip over any areas of the letter that need to be thickened.

Tips for stitching on multiple layers

Stitching through more than one layer of fabric is always tougher than stitching through a single layer. Cuffs usually have three layers: outer fabric, interfacing, and facing. Before transferring a design onto your fabric, test to see how easy it is to pass the needle and thread through your fabric. If the stitching is tough going, try **different sizes of needles** to find one that pulls through your fabric easily, use **thread conditioner,** or use a **needle puller** and a **thimble**.

I Do!

Splendid satin ribbons embroidered with silk threads are an exquisite way to express sweet sentiments on a wedding day. The ribbon can be tied around a floral bouquet, sewn onto the hem of an heirloom gown, or tied in a bow to decorate an elegant gift. A petite bow would be charming on the ring bearer's pillow. Embroidered ribbons add charisma to scrapbooks and cards as well, and can become a bookmark.

1 Copy the pattern and transfer it onto your ribbon.

2 Thread a fine crewel needle with a single strand of silk embroidery floss, and backstitch the entire outline of the design.

3 Thread a fine tapestry needle with a single strand of silk embroidery floss, and work the whipping step of the *whipped backstitch* over the entire design.

4 *Satin stitch* across the wide downstrokes of your letters with two strands of silk embroidery floss.

5 Use one strand of silk floss to whip over any areas of the letter that need to be thickened.

6 Stitch a *French knot* for the dot of the exclamation point.

You'll need...

Satin ribbon, 1½" (39 mm) wide, sky blue

Craft scissors, for cutting wired ribbon

Tools/materials for transferring the design

Crewel needle, fine

Silk embroidery floss: medium rose

Tapestry needle, fine

Embroidery scissors

More ideas...

amore

true Love

always

monogram

Mr. & Mrs.

Crewel Monogram

Cool, contemporary designs are attracting a whole new generation of needle artists to crewel work—traditional embroidery stitches with two-ply worsted wool yarn on linen. We used the fabulous dimensional effects of crewel embroidery to transform a ready-made pillow into sophisticated, expensive looking, custom décor. Pearl thread and cord trim outlines add the weight and substance that a large design requires. For your monogram, select home décor colors that coordinate or contrast with your pillow.

1 Trace the desired letter, and enlarge it to the desired size, using a copy machine. Transfer the design onto the fabric (see tips for pattern transfer on page 79).

2 Thread a chenille needle with two strands of green crewel yarn. *Backstitch* the entire design.

3 Thread a tapestry needle with two strands of green crewel yarn, and work the whipping step of the *whipped backstitches*.

4 *Satin stitch* across the wide downstrokes of your letters with the chenille needle and two strands of green crewel yarn.

5 Use one strand of green crewel yarn to whip over any areas of the letter that need to be thickened.

6 *Couch* a black pearl thread around the entire design using a single strand of black embroidery floss, threaded on a crewel needle, as the couching thread.

7 *Couch* a narrow black cord outline right next to the couched black pearl thread, using a single strand of black embroidery floss as the couching thread.

8 Lay a clean thick, white, terrycloth towel on your ironing board, and place the pillow top, embroidered side down, on the towel. The towel will prevent the embroidery from being flattened by the iron when you press the fabric. Cover the back of the embroidery with a dampened press cloth, and press with medium heat. Turn the pillow top right side up and iron only the areas around the design. Don't iron directly over the embroidery.

You'll need...

Pillow with removable cover

Tools/materials for transferring the design

Chenille needle, size 22

Wool crewel yarn: green

Tapestry needle, size 22

Cotton pearl thread, size 5: black

Cotton embroidery floss: black

Narrow cord trim: black

Embroidery scissors

Crewel needle, size 10

Iron and ironing board

Thick white terrycloth towel

Cotton press cloth

Tip for crossing lines

Parts of some letters look like they overlap—in reality they don't. You should **stop stitching** just before crossing another design line, then **start stitching** again on the other side. This keeps your stitches from piling up in an unsightly lump.

Bling

This tattoo flash extravaganza design looks outrageously complicated. Believe it or not, it's so easy that you can complete it with only two basic stitches. The stitching is sparked up with bugle beads and glitter paint. Show off your personal style by filling in the letters with rhinestones, sequins, beads, glitter, fabric paints, trims, bits of jewelry. But first, see page 75 for important tips on stitching with metallic thread.

1   Wash and iron the fabric.

2   Enlarge the pattern on page 57 and transfer it to your fabric.

3   Sparingly apply jewel glue to the bugle beads and adhere them to your fabric, following the photo for placement. Let the glue dry completely.

4   Put your fabric in the embroidery hoop.

5   Thread the embroidery needle with two strands of silver metallic embroidery thread, and *backstitch* the remaining lines

You'll need...

Tank top or t-shirt

Tools/materials for transferring the design

Jewel glue

Silver twisted bugle beads, 1" (2.5 cm) long

Large embroidery hoop

Crewel embroidery needle

Silver metallic embroidery thread

Thread conditioner

Tapestry needle

Beading needle

Embroidery scissors

Silver seed beads

Silver glitter acrylic paint

Textile medium

Fabric brushes: size 5/0 spotter and size 4 shader

Tips for stitching on T-shirts

Before embroidering a T-shirt, **iron** the area where you'll be stitching, and apply **spray starch.** The starching will add stability and make it easier to stitch through the fabric.

If the fabric is thin, use lightweight **fusible interfacing** as a stabilizer (page 82).

Embroidering on thin fabrics, stretchy fabrics, or fabrics with even a tiny amount of spandex in them can be challenging. Take a look at some of the **potential problems** and how to avoid them on pages 82 and 83.

of the design. Don't forget to use thread conditioner on metallic thread.

6   Thread the tapestry needle with two strands of silver metallic thread, and work the whipping step of the *whipped backstitch*.

7   Thread the beading needle with two strands of silver metallic thread, and stitch bugle beads in place, adding a seed bead at both ends of each bugle bead.

8   Apply a small drop of jewel glue onto each knot or loose thread on the wrong side of your embroidery.

9   Mix the silver glitter paint with the textile medium to create fabric paint, following the directions on the bottle of textile medium. Carefully paint along the inner edge of the outline using the spotter brush. Fill in the rest of the design using the shader brush.

Enlarge pattern 110%

Mom

Christmas stockings are traditionally personalized with names, so stitch one up for anybody who hasn't been too naughty. Use threads and embellishments in their favorite colors.

1 Enlarge the pattern and transfer it onto your fabric (see the tips on pages 79 and 80).

2 Thread the chenille needle with two strands of plum crewel yarn, and *backstitch* the outline of the entire design.

3 *Satin stitch* across the wide downstroke(s) of your letters with two strands of plum crewel yarn.

4 Thread the tapestry needle with one strand of plum crewel yarn, and work the whipping step of the *whipped backstitch* over the hairline strokes and flourishes of the letters.

5 Use two strands of plum crewel yarn to whip over any areas of the letters that need to be thickened.

6 Cut flower shapes from fleece fabric, and cut a tiny slit in the center of each. Cut ¼" (6 mm) strips of fleece 5" (12.7 cm) long for the stems. Thread a stem through the center of each flower, and tie a knot in the stem on the right side of the flower. Stitch a cluster of flowers to the cuff of the stocking. Stitch other flowers to the toe.

Enlarge pattern 125%

You'll need...

Plain Christmas stocking

Tools/materials for transferring the design

Chenille needle, size 22

Wool tapestry yarn: light plum

Tapestry needle, size 22

Embroidery scissors

Fleece

Tips for stitching "in hand"

When it's difficult or impractical to mount a project in a hoop you must embroider it "in hand." Be very careful to use a **delicate touch** as you're pulling the thread snug to your fabric. Keep your **thread tension consistent** and make each stitch the same size. Experienced stitchers say that it's better to stitch an entire area in **one sitting** because when you stop and start up again it is hard to match the tension of your stitches.

Girls

A logo script ending with a swash is so "team jersey." Attach this appliqué to a jacket, sweater, gym bag, lunch box, even a small canvas for a door decoration or wall hanging.

1   Wash and iron your fabric.

2   Thread the chenille needle with light green pearl thread, and *blanket stitch* around the neck and sleeve openings. (Don't use an embroidery hoop for this step.)

3   Enlarge the pattern and transfer it onto the felted wool. Mount the felted wool in the embroidery hoop.

4   Thread the chenille needle with white pearl thread, and outline all of the lettering with *split stitches*.

You'll need...

T-shirt or tank top

Iron and ironing board

Chenille needle, size 22

Cotton pearl thread, size 3: light green, white, and raspberry

Tools/materials for transferring the design

Felted wool, raspberry

Embroidery hoop

Fabric shears

Fabric glue

Crewel embroidery needle, fine

Cotton embroidery floss: raspberry

Embroidery scissors

Tips for using fabric glue

To apply fabric glue to a large surface, use a wide, flat **artist paint-brush.** Just be sure to rinse the brush right after use.

Appliqués attached with fabric glue can be safely **laundered.** Read and follow the instructions on the glue bottle.

If you've glued the appliqué to a hard surface such as a lunch box, simply attach the **outline of pearl thread** with glue.

5   Using the same needle and white pearl thread, fill in the spaces with rows of *chain stitching.*

6   Remove the felt from the hoop and trim the felt to within ¼" (6 mm) of the stitching, using fabric shears.

7   Iron the front of the tee where the felt embroidery will be attached. Let the tee remain lying smooth and flat. Spread a thin, even layer of fabric glue over the back of the felt, and adhere it to the tee. Allow the fabric glue to dry completely.

8   For a finishing touch, *couch* an outline around the entire appliqué, stitching on the tee. Use a single strand of raspberry embroidery floss, threaded on a crewel needle, as the couching thread and the raspberry pearl thread as the laid thread.

Enlarge pattern 110%

Tickled Pink

A mom-to-be would love this darling onesie to bring to the hospital with her so she can dress her newborn in a unique homecoming tog. If you don't know the sex of the new baby or if the baby is a boy, switch colors and pick a phrase that's just right for your special little one. The lettering for this project is layered, one style over the other. It's fun to add trims that mirror the words you stitch, like this fuzzy, tickling yarn that we couched around the sleeve openings.

1 Wash and iron the fabric.

2 Copy the design for the word "PINK" (page 67) and transfer it onto your fabric.

3 Mix the pink paint with the textile medium to create fabric paint, following the directions on the bottle of textile medium. Carefully paint the outline of each letter, using the spotter brush. Fill in the rest of the letters, using the shader brush. Let the painted letters dry completely.

You'll need...

Newborn-sized onesie

Tools/materials for transferring the design

Pink fabric paint or acrylic paint and textile medium

Fabric painting brushes: size 5/0 spotter and size 4 shader

Embroidery hoop, large enough to fit entire design

Embroidery scissors

Pearlescent embroidery floss

Chenille needle, size 22

Crewel embroidery needle

Thread conditioner

Fabric glue

More ideas...

itsy BITSY
little ANGEL
new BORN
bundle of JOY
precious ONE

--- --- --- ---

Tip for couching

To control your laid thread when you are stitching with the couching thread, pin a safety pin off to the side of your work, and wrap the laid thread around it.

4 Trace the word "tickled" onto tracing paper. Transfer the design to your fabric right across the painted letters.

5 Put the fabric in an embroidery hoop. It's important that the hoop doesn't touch the painted letters. The hoop could permanently dent or crack your paint.

6 Cut an 18" (46 cm) length of the pearlescent floss. (You'll need enough floss to spell out the entire word "tickled.") Thread the chenille needle with all six strands of the pearlescent floss–don't separate or untwist the threads! Knot the end of the thread.

7 Plunge the needle through to the front of the design at the beginning point of the letter "t." Pull the entire thread through to the front. This thread is now your laid thread.

8 Thread the crewel needle with a single strand of pearlescent floss to use as the couching thread. Use thread conditioner on your couching thread. *Couch* the laid thread down along the whole word.

9 When you're finished couching the thread down, plunge the chenille needle through to the back at the end point of the letter "d". Pull all of the remaining thread through to the back and tie a knot. Apply a small dot of fabric glue over each knot.

tickled

PiNK

Say Cheese

It's easy to alter this fanciful tag project to ID lots of your stuff. Create your own version of this tag for a purse handle, gift package, zipper pull, or even make a tiny cell phone tag with "hello" on it. If you make a luggage tag, don't use your name (for safety and security reasons). The tag is so unique anyway, that you'll recognize your suitcase coming along on the luggage carousel in an instant.

1   Transfer the pattern onto the felted wool.

2   Put the felted wool into an embroidery hoop.

3   *Backstitch* the word "Say" with two strands of light green embroidery floss.

4   Thread a crewel needle with two strands of black embroidery floss. Start the letter "c" on the dot by stitching a *French knot.* Don't cut the thread.

5   Continuing with the same thread, *backstitch* the word "cheese."

6   Thread a tapestry needle with two strands of black embroidery floss and do the whipping step of the *whipped backstitch.*

7   Trim the embroidered felted wool to fit into your tag opening. Slip it into the opening. Secure it with a few touches of glue on the back.

8   Tie 10" (25.5 cm) pieces of ribbon and black trim through the hole in the tag.

9   Thread another piece of ribbon through a clear button, and tie the ribbon into a knot. Secure the button over the hole in the tag with a drop of jewel glue.

You'll need...

Lemon felted wool, just large enough to fit into a small embroidery hoop

Tools/materials for transferring the design

Small embroidery hoop

Cotton embroidery floss: light green and black

Crewel needle

Embroidery scissors

Tapestry needle

Fabric shears

Luggage tag

Fabric glue

½ yd. (0.5 m) black and white gingham ribbon, ¼" (7 mm) wide

Black trim

Clear two-hole button

Jewel glue

Smile

Here's another way to spiff up an ordinary tag, whether it is a purchased luggage tag, a gift tag, or a tag you make yourself from leather or craft foam. Wouldn't a stitched tag make an adorable scrapbook page embellishment?

1 Transfer the pattern onto the felted wool.

2 Put the felted wool into an embroidery hoop.

3 Thread a crewel needle with two strands of light green embroidery floss. *Chain stitch* the "smile" lettering.

4 Stitch on a charm or little button for the dot over the "i" or make a *French knot.*

5 Place your tag over the stitched lettering, and trace the outline of the tag on the felted wool. Cut out the felted wool shape.

6 Thread a chenille needle with orange-red pearl thread. *Blanket stitch* around the outside of the tag.

7 Spread a thin, even film of fabric glue over the entire back of your tag, and adhere the felted wool.

8 Tie a length of grosgrain ribbon through the tag hole.

9 Thread orange-red pearl thread through a clear button, tie the thread into a tiny bow. Secure the button over the hole in the tag with a drop of jewel glue.

Smile

You'll need...

Sunflower felted wool, just large enough to fit into your small embroidery hoop

Tools/materials for transferring the design

Small embroidery hoop

Crewel needle

Cotton embroidery floss: light green

Embroidery scissors

Star charm

Luggage tag

Fabric shears

Chenille needle, size 22

Cotton pearl thread, size 5: orange-red

Fabric glue

½ yd. (0.5 m) light green ribbon, ¼" (7 mm) wide

Clear two-hole button

Jewel glue

It's EZ When You Know How

GET READY

Embroidery doesn't require a lot of expensive materials or machines. Basically, you need something to stitch on, threads, needles, and some notions. The right tools and materials can make projects go a lot easier and faster and will help you achieve better results, too. Let's go shopping!

FABRICS

There's a world of fabric out there for you to embroider. Pull something from your closet, a thrift store (great old linens), or the sale rack. (You can stitch on paper, too; more on that later.) Some fabrics are easier to stitch on than others, but with a few pointers and a little practice, you can get great results on almost any fabric.

For your very first project, pick a solid-color fabric with a stable, even weave, such as an all-cotton bandanna, linen napkin, or tea towel. A plain fabric will help you see the way the stitches are being formed. Also, start with a flat object or piece of fabric, not something like jeans. When you're happy with the way your stitches are turning out, try embroidering on printed fabric.

Embellished T-shirts are so hot, you have to do one. Luckily, standard cotton tees are a good choice for embroidery because they have a smooth knit with no ridges. Knit fabric is trickier to embroider than woven fabric because it stretches. It helps to stabilize the fabric with lightweight interfacing (see page 82). We don't recommend stitching over stretchy fabrics or fabrics with large ridges.

Sheets, pillowcases, and other linens are begging for embroidery. However, you'll need to experiment with needles and threads to discover which combinations work best for your linens, especially those with high thread counts. In general, the higher the thread count, the finer the needle and thread.

Denim is a natural choice for updated embroidery designs. Although it is tough to work the needle in and out of this dense fabric, with the right needle, a needle puller, and a few tips, you can do it. When working on denim:

- Pick an area on the garment where you will stitch through one layer of fabric. If you want to embellish a yoke, cuff, or collar, you will be stitching through two or more layers and doing some serious tugging on the needle. (In fact, stitching through more than one layer is usually more difficult, whatever the fabric.)

- Use the smallest needle you can thread two strands of embroidery floss into, and choose embroidery floss rather than pearl cotton.

- Since denim can be extra tough, sometimes it's easier to support the fabric with your fingers rather than using an embroidery hoop. Try it and see which works better for you.

Felt is the quintessential fabric choice for quickie projects and appliqué because its cut edges won't ravel or fray. That means you can just cut it and get on with your crafting. That said, if you want a finished look, blanket stitching (page 96) is a very traditional edge trim for felt shapes.

All felts are not the same. Here's some good-to-know info:

- Craft felt is composed of nonwoven synthetic fibers that are treated with heat, pressure, and a chemical bonding agent to mat them into a sheet of fabric. Craft felt is very inexpensive and comes in a wide range of colors—we've even seen some with glitter. You can buy craft felt in precut rectangles in a craft department or by-the-yard from a bolt in the fabric department. It's sold for basic crafty uses and is a good choice for projects that won't get wear and tear or won't ever be laundered, or when cost, not longevity is a consideration.

- Wool felt is composed of nonwoven wool and other fibers that are matted together when they are processed with heat, pressure, and chemicals. You'll find wool felt on bolts in the fabric department. Wool felt is stronger than craft felt, has a nicer "feel" to it, and also costs more.

- Felted wool is made from a woven wool fabric that has been processed with heat, friction, and pressure to make the fibers shrink and wrap tighter around each other, resulting in a dense, sturdy fabric that won't shrink, fray, or stretch out of shape. It is more expensive than wool felt, but great for special projects. Look for felted wool in quilt shops and fabric departments.

- You can substitute felted wool or wool felt for craft felt whenever you want to "upgrade" your project, but never use craft felt where felted wool or wool felt is specifically called for.

Before you start a project, wash whatever you're going to stitch on to remove sizing and prevent shrinking and puckering later. Follow the guidelines for laundering on the manufacturer's care label. Press the fabric or item with a clean iron, from the wrong side whenever possible. Ironing fabric before cutting helps you cut it more accurately. Pressing and starching the fabric before stitching gives you a smoother, more stable surface, making stitching easier and better looking.

THREADS

Every color imaginable! Sheen and sparkle! Choosing and working with threads is pure enjoyment.

You'll want to buy good thread. DMC and Anchor are high-quality, reliable brands that produce great results. These brands are colorfast, which means they will not bleed onto the fabric when they are wet. Quality brands of thread won't shrink and cause your project to pucker. Floss and thread are inexpensive. Avoid "bargain" brands that can give you much more trouble than you bargained for.

PEARL THREAD (1). The quintessential thread for beginners. Everybody loves cotton pearl thread's lustrous sheen and vast color selection. It comes in three weights, #3, #5, and #8—the highest number being the lightest weight—and is tightly twisted so you use it as one thread. You can't and shouldn't try to separate strands.

SIX-STRAND EMBROIDERY FLOSS. Floss is available in lots of fibers: cotton (2), linen (3), and rayon (4), to name a few. It comes in almost every color you can imagine, even variegated (5) and unusual hand-dyed colors. When you separate floss into individual strands and recombine them, you can achieve a variety of effects depending on the number of strands used. One strand produces very fine lines and delicate details. All six strands can be used to create thick, bold stitches.

METALLIC THREAD, SPECIALTY THREADS, AND OTHER FUN FIBERS (6). These are the icing on the cake! When you feel confident about your skill with cotton pearl thread and floss, practice with silk (yum!) thread for a while before you try to work with metallic or other specialty threads. Silk is slippery, but it's a lot easier to handle than many other specialty threads. Metallic and specialty threads tend to fray, untwist, tangle, or snag after a while. The first line of defense is to use short lengths of thread. Use a slightly larger needle than you would normally, so it makes a hole big enough not to "rough up" the thread. As soon as you notice that the thread is looking thinner, frayed, or worn, end that thread and begin again with a fresh thread. Despite their trickiness, don't hesitate to embroider with these sweet threads. The more you stitch with them, the more you'll love using them. Use a thread conditioner to keep things moving along smoothly.

CREWEL WOOL YARN (7) looks like two very thin strands of wool twisted together, but it's not meant to be untwisted or divided. Use it just as it comes in the skein, as one strand. One strand of crewel wool is similar in thickness and coverage to two strands of cotton embroidery floss or one strand of size 8 pearl thread.

TAPESTRY WOOL (8) is a thick wool thread that is usually used for needlepoint. It is heavier and sturdier than crewel wool and can be used in embroidery projects as a laid thread for couching.

Before you know it, you'll have lots of threads and flosses. What's the best way to keep everything organized so you can find what you want for your next project? We keep each color of floss or thread in an individual, snack size, resealable plastic bag. Write the color number on the outside of the bag with a fine-tip permanent marker. We like to save the label with the color number and brand information in the bag as well. The plastic bags keep your threads clean, dry, and fuzz free and will keep small humans and pet friends safe. (We learned about this danger the hard way after paying $1,000 to have embroidery floss surgically removed from our cat Toby's stomach!)

When you've amassed a collection of little plastic bags of thread, organize them by color into a small storage box. Plastic shoe boxes with snap-on lids or photo storage boxes work well for this. Label each box with the colors that it contains. Storage units with shallow drawers are handy for storing thread, too.

NEEDLES

The right needle makes embroidering delightful; the wrong needle makes it harder than it has to be. A needle's job is to make a hole in the fabric that the thread can pass through easily, so the thread doesn't drag and wear down. If the needle is too narrow, the thread will fray and break. If the needle is too wide, you can have trouble getting it through your fabric, it might leave holes, and your stitches will look sloppy.

Needles don't cost a lot, so buy the best quality you can find. Cheap needles can have burrs on them, and they often bend, snap, and rust easily. It's time to throw out a needle when it feels rough or won't pull through your fabric smoothly.

The right size of needle depends on the size of the thread. The correct size needle should be slightly wider at the eye (the hole for the thread) than the thickness of your

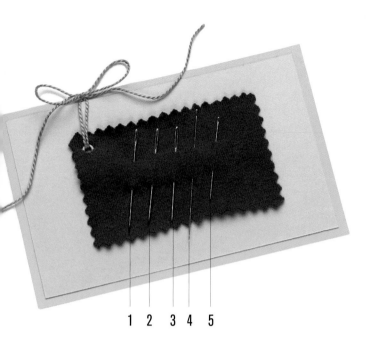

1   2   3   4   5

thread. For help selecting the size of needle, see the project instructions or the chart below.

Store needles in a pincushion, wool/felt needle book, or wooden tube needle case to keep them sharp, clean, dry, and free from corrosion.

CREWEL OR EMBROIDERY NEEDLES (1). These have a sharp point for piercing fabric. They have an elongated oval eye that makes it easy to thread stranded embroidery floss. Some companies use the name "crewel" on their packaging for embroidery needles.

CHENILLE NEEDLES (2). These also have a sharp point that will pierce through fabric and other threads, but they are thicker and longer and have a longer, bigger eye than crewel needles. The large eye allows you to thread pearl cotton, yarn, thick threads, or stranded embroidery floss.

TAPESTRY NEEDLES (3). Similar to chenille needles, these needles have a blunt tip. They are used for stitches worked in the surface threads, such as the whipping on running and backstitches or the weaving on woven and double-woven backstitches. Tapestry needles are also used for most paper crafts.

Crewel or Embroidery Needle Sizes	Floss Strands	Tapestry and Chenille Needle Sizes	Floss Strands
10	one strand of six-stranded floss	26	one or two strands of six-stranded floss
8	three strands of six-stranded floss	24	three or four strands of six-stranded floss
3	six strands of six-stranded floss	22	six strands of six-stranded floss
6	#5 pearl cotton	22	#5 pearl cotton

BEADING NEEDLES (4). Longer and thinner than ordinary sewing needles, beading needles arc about the same diameter the whole length, with a tiny round eye that beads can easily pass over.

SHARPS (5). These are general sewing needles. They have small round eyes and sharp points.

CUTTING TOOLS

You'll need some simple cutting tools. Shears have a small handle for your thumb and a larger handle for your other fingers. Scissors have same-sized handles. If you're stitching on paper, you'll need a few special tools; see the section on paper (page 103).

CRAFT SCISSORS AND SHEARS (1). Have a pair of these on hand, too. They're for cutting paper, cardstock, and other things that you shouldn't cut with your embroidery scissors or fabric shears.

EMBROIDERY SCISSORS (2). With small blades and very sharp, tiny, pointed tips, embroidery scissors are used for trimming threads and snipping out bad stitches. Never use them for anything else. Keep them in a sheath or case to protect them and yourself.

FABRIC SHEARS (3). These should only be used for cutting fabric and threads; they will become dull if they are used to cut paper.

TIP

You might want to label your fabric shears "FABRIC ONLY" with a permanent marker so nobody ruins them by mistake.

1

2

3

WATER-ERASABLE MARKER (4). Use with transfer mesh, stencil, or template. Marks can be washed away with a few drops of water.

AIR-ERASABLE MARKER (5). Use with transfer mesh, stencil, or template. Marks will disappear after about 48 hours, so use this method when you will be able to complete your project in this time.

WAX-FREE DRESSMAKER'S TRACING PAPER (6). This comes in sheets; colors are shown in the small samples. Tape the tracing paper facedown on the right side of the fabric; tape the pattern faceup over the tracing paper. Trace the pattern with a ballpoint pen so you can see whether you have traced all the lines. Marks not covered by embroidery can be brushed away or erased.

LIGHT BOX (NOT SHOWN). You can place your fabric over the pattern on a light box or bright window and trace directly onto the fabric, using a marking pencil or pen.

The best method for transferring a big pattern onto a large surface is to first trace the pattern onto a transfer material. This can be a fine transparent fabric (like organdy or tulle) that allows you to see the placement of your pattern. Our favorite transfer material is Stitch Witchery (normally used as an iron-on adhesive) because it doesn't shift around on the fabric. Position the transfer material over your fabric and trace over the design again with an erasable fabric marker or chalk pencil.

The heat transfer pencil is often the best method for transferring patterns to knit fabrics. Usually the marks from iron-on transfer pencils are permanent. Be precise in tracing your pattern so you don't end up with unwanted marks that will show on your finished embroidery. Work your stitches right on top of the pattern marks, completely covering them.

HOOPS

Fabric mounted in an embroidery hoop is easier to work with. A hoop holds your fabric tight from all directions while you're stitching. It helps you keep the size of your stitches even and keeps you from pulling your stitches too tight, which makes the fabric pucker.

Embroidery hoops come in an assortment of styles and sizes. Wood and plastic hoops have an adjustable screw on the outer ring; metal ones just have a spring. Whenever you can, select a hoop large enough to fit the whole design so the fabric won't have to be moved during stitching. The pressure of the rings can crush stitches when the hoop has to be moved around to the other areas of the design.

To help keep fabric taut and to protect delicate fabric, wrap cotton twill tape around the inner ring. Secure the end with a few stitches. If your fabric is very delicate, or you need to place the hoop on stitches, wrap the top hoop, too.

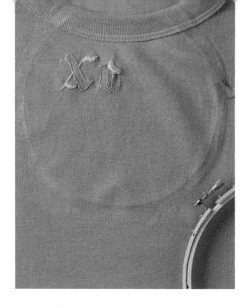

TIP

Take your project out of the
hoop when you aren't working
on it to prevent permanent dents
or distortions in your fabric.

Here's how to put the fabric in a hoop:

1. Lay the smaller, inner ring on a flat surface. Center your design, right side up, over the inner ring.

2. Lay the outer adjustable ring over the fabric. It's a good idea to position the screw at the top of your project so your thread doesn't get caught on it as you stitch. Lefties locate the screw on the right side of the top, righties on the left side of the top. Press the outer ring down with even pressure until it is secure.

3. Tighten the screw until the outer ring fits snugly over the inner ring and fabric.

Gently pull the fabric evenly from all sides until it is taut but not too tight. The fabric should feel and sound like a drumhead when you flick it with your fingertip.

STABILIZING KNITS

Embroidered tees are great, but some problems can develop if you're not careful. Hoops can stretch out the fabric or leave a permanent ring around your design. Because the fabric is so stretchy and often thin, your stitches can cause unsightly puckers. Bonding a lightweight fusible interfacing to the back of the fabric before you start stitching will make a huge difference in the quality of your embroidery. Our favorite interfacing for this is Pellon Easy Knit.

On very thin fabrics you might be able to detect the outline of the stabilizer through your fabric. With a little planning, you can use that effect to your advantage and add a subtle texture to your design. Cut the stabilizer into a shape—a heart, star, oval, or circle—that is slightly larger than your design. Round off any sharp points and fuse the

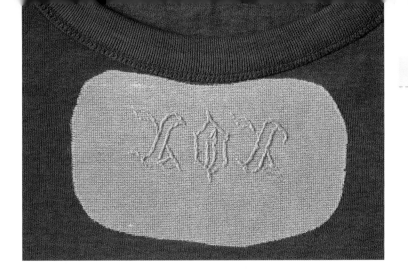

TIP

Embroidered areas can feel itchy against your skin, especially if you've used metallic thread or have lots of knots. We've found that a patch of Easy Knit fused over the back of the finished design is a great "anti-itch" remedy!

patch behind the area you are going to embroider. To secure it even more, add a line of stitching around the perimeter of the stabilizer with a single strand of embroidery floss. Match the floss to your fabric for a subtle effect or, for a bit more obvious impression, repeat a color from the design. Cool!

Sometimes, after repeated laundering, the stabilizer might detach from your fabric in spots. To prevent that, make sure to follow the manufacturer's instructions exactly. We've been told that avoiding fabric softeners will help prevent this problem. If your stabilizer does become loose, though, simply iron it back into place.

GET SET

PREPARE THE FLOSS OR THREAD

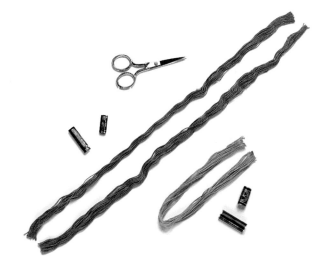

When you open a new skein:

1. Remove the labels and save the label that has the color number on it.

2. Untwist the pearl thread. Lay out the pearl thread or floss into an oval shape.

3. Cut through the pearl thread strands at both ends of the oval, so you have two bundles of 12" (30.5 cm) pieces. Cut through the floss at only one end of the oval, so you have one bundle of 12" (30.5 cm) pieces.

Often you need to separate one, two, or more strands of floss from a six-strand length. To keep them from tangling, remove just one strand of floss at a time. After cutting the floss into 12" (30.5 cm) pieces (page 83), hold the top of one piece in your hand. Use the other hand to separate one end from the group. Pull that strand straight up and out from the rest. The remaining strands will probably bunch up as you remove it, but you can easily smooth them back in place. Repeat the process to remove each individual strand that you need.

Floss should be straightened before stitching to produce smooth, even stitches. Straightening is also an effective way to revive threads that are creased from being tightly wound on a cardboard or plastic bobbin or for threads that have been crumpled up. Slightly moisten each individual strand with a drop of water; use the tips of your fingers (or a small, damp sponge) to smooth out and spread the moisture along the length of the strand. The strand should be barely moist, not wet, and should dry completely before you thread your needle.

You can blend strands to create customized colors and special effects. First, straighten each individual strand. Then lay out the straightened strands with the ends aligned, and smooth them out along their length. Don't twist the strands. Skim the group as one combined strand across the surface of a thread conditioner. Thread your needle and trim both ends even. Beginners might find it easier to start stitching by tying a small tight knot at the end of the combined strand to help hold all of the strands together.

THREAD THE NEEDLE

Through the ages, millions of needles have been threaded by people who put the end of the thread into their mouths to wet the tip. Many discerning needleworkers use a small sponge and water for moistening thread. Either way will work. Once the tip of the thread is moistened, use your embroidery scissors to snip the tip, either at an angle or straight across. Pinch the tip, aim, and thread it through the needle eye.

Having a little trouble? Try threading the needle from its other side. Occasionally, a needle eye is smaller on one side than the other. Still no luck? Don't get frustrated. Try using a time-saving and very inexpensive needle threader (page 78).

TIPS FOR GOOD STITCHES

Now you're ready to start stitching! Use a straight up-and-down stabbing motion, pulling the thread all the way through to the front or back with each motion. It will help you to keep your stitches and tension (how tight you pull the thread) even.

Aim for equal-sized stitches and consistent tension. Your stitches should be flat against the fabric, neither loopy and loose nor tight and scrunching up the fabric. Here are some tips:

- Put the "how to" illustration of the stitch you're learning where you can see it, and refer to it as you take each step.

- Before starting a project, try the stitches that are new to you on a scrap of fabric until you're happy about the way they look. Almost everyone needs a little practice.

- Start all of your stitches on the wrong side of the fabric.

- Use a hoop whenever you can.

- The normal motions of stitching often cause the thread to tangle. When your thread becomes twisted, let the needle hang down and dangle freely until the thread unwinds itself. It's a good idea to do this every once in a while even if you don't think you need to.

KNOTS AND TAILS

For projects where the underside of the embroidery will never be seen, it's okay to tie a small knot in the end of the thread to anchor the first stitch. Do this by wrapping the thread end once around the tip of your index finger. Then, using your thumb, roll the thread off your finger, twisting it into a small knot. When the thread gets too short or you finish a stitching line, pull the needle to the underside and take a couple tiny stitches where they won't show before cutting the thread.

There are some projects, such as napkins or a handkerchief, where people will see both sides of your embroidery. Here are ways to start without knots and hide the tails so the wrong side looks almost as good as the right side.

For a knot-free beginning, use a "waste knot," following these steps:

1. Make a knot at the end of your thread.

2. Insert the needle on the right side of the fabric about 2" (5 cm) from your starting point on the pattern line where your stitching will be heading.

3. Bring the needle up from the wrong side of the fabric at your starting point. The knot will be on the right side and the thread will trail under the pattern line on the wrong side.

4. Work your stitches, crossing over the thread on the wrong side to secure it.

5. Just before you reach the knot, snip it off. That's where the name "waste" knot comes from.

If you already have some stitching done, simply weave your needle under the back (wrong side) of a few stitches of the same or similar color before bringing the needle to the right side at the start of a line. To hide the tail at the end of a line, weave the needle under several stitches of the same or similar color and snip off the remaining bit of the tail close to the fabric. When the stitches are too large or loose to hold the thread securely, make a few backstitches through the threads on the wrong side of the fabric.

TIP

Nobody's perfect! To recover from a bad stitch or two, simply remove the needle from your thread. Then, working from the wrong side of the fabric, use the needle to loosen the thread and undo the stitch. Rethread your needle with the same thread, redo the stitch, and get back to work. To correct more than a few bad stitches, use your embroidery scissors to clip the stitches on the wrong side of the fabric, taking care not to cut the fabric. Use tweezers to pick out the stitches from the right side. Pull free a 2" (5 cm) tail of thread, and thread it back onto the needle on the wrong side. Weave the tail under the back of some of the remaining good stitches.

KEEP IT CLEAN

TIP

You accidentally prick your finger and get a drop of blood on your fabric; what do you do? Don't let it dry. Immediately cut a length of light-colored thread, roll it into a ball, and put it in your mouth, wetting it with your own saliva. Lay a paper towel or white terry-cloth towel under the embroidery to act as a blotter. Then rub the wet ball of thread over the blood spot. The enzymes in your saliva react with your own blood to dissolve it. Follow by rinsing the spot with cold water. Press a clean white towel on the wet spot to help it dry quickly.

Most embroidered work deserves some special treatment when it comes to cleaning. Do read and follow the care instructions that come with the threads/fibers and fabrics/clothing that you buy. Silk or wool threads and fabrics, for instance, may require dry cleaning. Consider the care requirements and how often your item will be cleaned when you're making fabric and thread selections. For items that are likely to need cleaning often—kids' things, jeans, or a tee—use materials that are sturdy (like 100% cotton) and will hold up to repeated laundering. For example, you wouldn't want to use silk or wool threads on a burp cloth, but they're perfect for a monogram on a sweater for your mom. You get the idea!

If only part of your embroidered design needs cleaning, try this spot-cleaning method first:

1. Spray the area with tepid water and a tiny dab of mild soap.

2. Brush the spot with a clean, soft toothbrush.

3. Rinse it well and pat the spot dry with a clean white towel.

4. If your item looks cleaned up, stop there. Less is more when it comes to washing embellishments.

If things get really dirty, you'll have to wash them. Most embroidered projects should be hand washed, especially projects that have glued on pompoms, rhinestones, beads, or charms because it's very likely that those decorations will be rubbed off or ruined during a machine wash or spin cycle. We recommend hand washing with your actual hands. Some washing machines have a very delicate or hand-wash cycle; try them at your own risk. Use mild soap and tepid water.

Embellishments get squished up, torn off, and destroyed in dryers, so take it easy on your embroidery. Lay your project flat, smooth it out (give the embroidery a gentle tug in each direction until it looks just like it did the day it was embroidered) and allow it to air dry.

FINISHING TOUCH

This special ironing method is a great finishing touch for all of your embroidery—it's the seasoned stitcher's secret to getting that desirable 3-D look that pops! Do this for all of your embroidered projects. Follow steps 2 to 5 after every laundering.

1. First be sure that your fabric is perfectly clean. Remove any pattern marks from your fabric, following the manufacturer's directions for the transfer product you used.

2. Lay a clean, thick, white terrycloth towel on your ironing board and place the embroidery face down over it. The towel prevents the embroidery from being flattened by the iron when you press the fabric.

3. Spray a light mist of spray starch over the back of the embroidery. Cover the back of the embroidery with a damp press cloth.

4. Lightly press with medium heat, moving from the center of the embroidery out toward the edges.

5. Take the towel off of the ironing board. Then flip the embroidery right side up and carefully iron only the areas around the embroidery. Never iron directly over the embroidery.

STITCH

Here are instructions for all the stitches used in these projects. Don't worry that you have to learn them all right away. In fact, you can make lots of fabulous designs with only one simple stitch. When you're ready for more, though, there are many easy stitches that create special effects for your projects.

EXCLUSIVE TIP FOR LEFTIES: If these embroidery stitch illustrations are confusing you, use a computer to reverse them so you'll have a mirror image copy. (Or take them to a copy shop and ask them to make mirror images for you.) Refer to your copies while you're learning new stitches. The mirror images will help you visualize the positioning for your needle and thread.

STRAIGHT STITCH

creates a little dash

Bring the needle up to the right side of the fabric at your starting point. Insert the needle the desired distance from the starting point; then pull it to the back of the fabric. That's it.

Cross-stitch is simply one diagonal straight stitch across another, with the stitches crossing in the center. For long lines of cross-stitches, work all the diagonal stitches in one direction and then turn around and work the stitches in the other direction. The cross-stitches in this book are free-form, unlike counted cross-stitches that require a chart or special even-weave fabric.

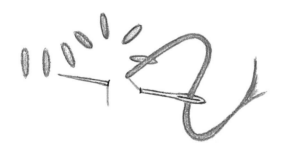

RUNNING STITCH

creates a broken dash-space-dash line

Bring the needle up to the right side of the fabric at your starting point. Push the needle in and out of the fabric along the pattern line, leaving a space between each stitch. Keep the stitches an even size and tension for a consistent look.

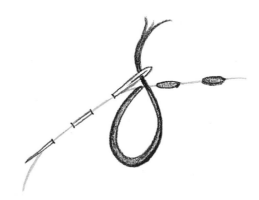

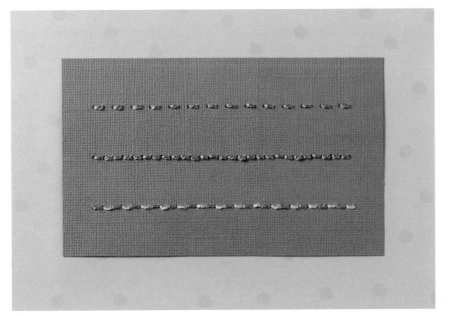

Top to bottom:
running stitch,
double running stitch,
alternate double
running stitch

DOUBLE RUNNING STITCH

creates a solid line of end-to-end dashes; you can use a different color for each line of stitches to make a solid line of alternating colored dashes

Stitch a line of evenly spaced running stitches. Using the same holes, stitch another row of running stitches, filling in the empty spaces left by the first line of stitches.

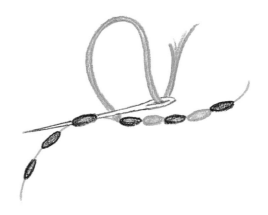

WHIPPED RUNNING STITCH

creates a solid, raised, narrow, twisted line

Stitch a base row of running stitches. Thread a tapestry needle with the "whipping" thread, and bring the needle up to the right side at the starting point of the base row of running stitches. Lace the tapestry needle under a running stitch, whip the thread over it, then lace the thread under the next running stitch. Repeat.

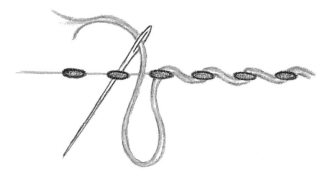

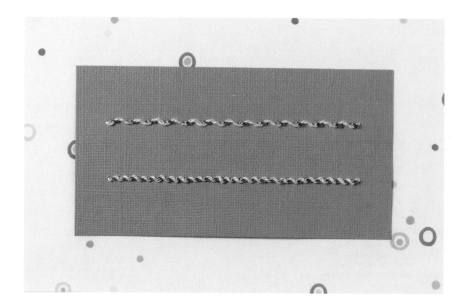

Top to bottom:
whipped running stitch,
whipped double
running stitch

WHIPPED DOUBLE RUNNING STITCH

creates a solid, raised, twisted line that looks like a small cord

Make a base line of double running stitches. Begin the whipping step at the starting point of the base row. Use a tapestry needle to lace under a stitch, whip the thread over it, then lace the thread under the following running stitch.

SATIN STITCH

very closely placed, side-by-side, straight stitches; used to fill shapes

Bring the thread up to the right side of your fabric precisely on the pattern line. Insert the needle straight across the shape, on the opposite side. Bring the needle out again as close as possible to the end of the first stitch. Insert the needle into the fabric straight across the shape in the opposite direction to form the next satin stitch. Repeat to fill the shape.

To pad satin stitches: Stitch split stitches (page 92) around the outline of the shape; then fill in the shape with small running stitches (page 83) to create a base. Use either straight or diagonal satin stitches from pattern line to pattern line over the outline to create a raised, padded look.

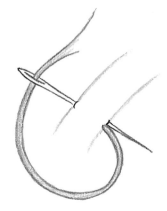

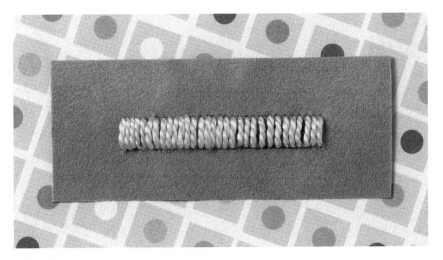

Satin stitch

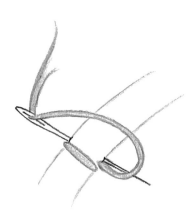

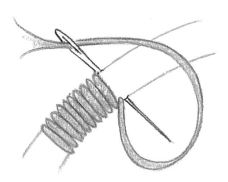

COUCHING

tiny stitches from one thread hold another thread in place

The thread that is sewn down is called the laid thread. The couching thread is the thread that sews the laid thread into place. Use a large chenille needle to bring the laid thread (whatever you're wanting to couch down) up to the front of the fabric at your starting point. Secure the laid thread onto the pattern line with pins or a tiny bit of fabric glue. Where you want to end the couching, "plunge" the laid thread through to the wrong side of the fabric. Secure the ends of the laid thread on the wrong side of the fabric with a few stitches from the couching thread. Bring the needle threaded with the couching thread up very close to the laid thread. Insert the needle down on the opposite side of the laid thread to make a stitch perpendicular to it. Bring the needle up into position for another perpendicular stitch. Take evenly spaced stitches over the laid thread until you reach its end. When you're finished stitching, dab a tiny drop of fabric glue onto the tails of the couching thread.

Couching

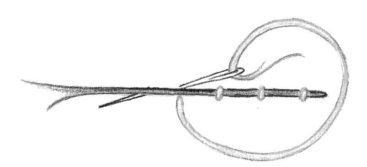

CORAL STITCH

creates a solid dash-knot-dash line

Bring the needle up to the right side of the fabric at your starting point. Make a tiny perpendicular stitch (through just a few threads of the fabric) across your pattern line. Keep the needle in the fabric; don't pull the thread through yet. Loop the thread over and under the needle tip. Then pull the thread through the loop, forming a knot.

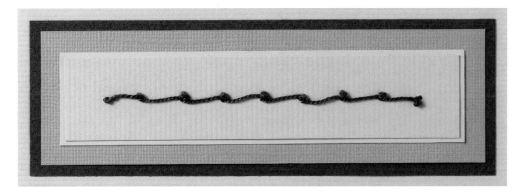

Coral stitch

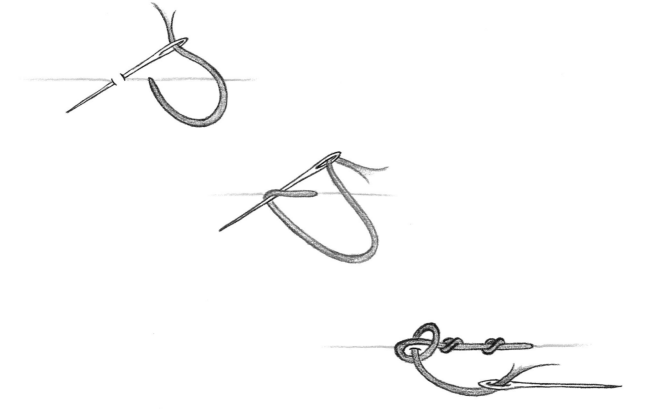

CHAIN STITCH

looks like a chain

Bring the needle up to the right side of the fabric at your starting point. Hold the thread toward you with your free thumb, take a stitch into the same hole where the thread was brought up, forming a small loop. Bring the needle up through the fabric where you want the end of the stitch but do not pull the thread through yet. Bring the needle out and over the loop. Use your free hand to guide the thread around the needle making a second loop overlapping the first one. Repeat.

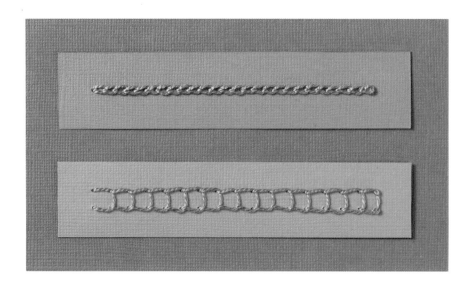

Top to bottom:
chain stitch,
square chain stitch

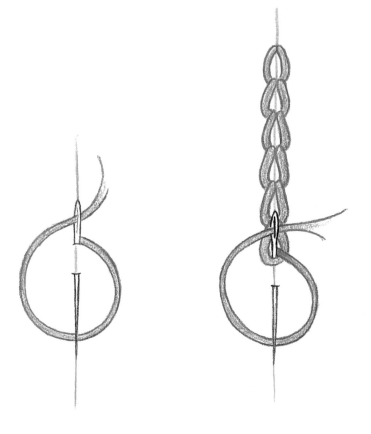

SQUARE CHAIN STITCH

creates a wide "ladder" looking stitch that can be laced with ribbon or other fibers

Draw two parallel lines where you want to stitch. You can use a line of stitching that is already on a garment as one of the guidelines, or stitch across a seam that has two parallel lines of stitching. You'll be stitching downward between the two parallel guidelines.

Bring the needle up to the right side of the fabric at your starting point on the left line. Insert the needle on the right line, directly across from your starting point; then in the same motion, bring the needle out under the starting point on the left line. *Don't pull the needle through yet. Loop the thread under the needle tip, then pull the thread through, but don't pull the thread tight. Leave a loop that you can insert the needle into to form the next stitch. Insert the needle into the right line, directly across from the emerging thread. Bring your needle up on the left line underneath the emerging thread. Repeat from * to the end of the line.

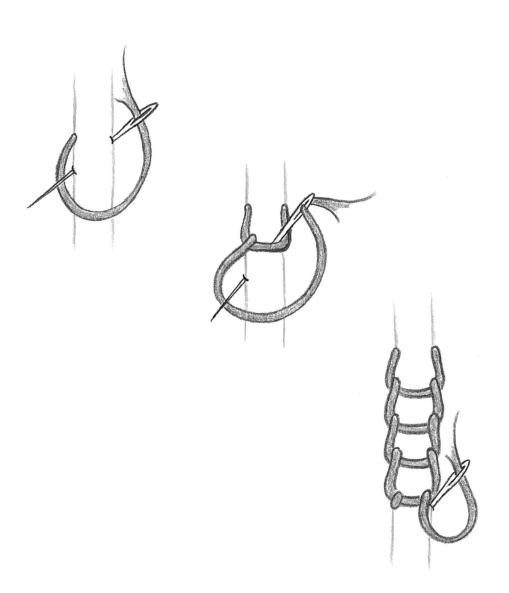

BLANKET STITCH

is often used as an embellishment and to secure the edges of appliqués

Insert the needle from the right side of the fabric through to the back. Bring the needle up while holding the loop of thread with your left thumb. Make a vertical stitch, bringing the needle out over the loop made by the thread. Pull the needle through until the blanket stitch is snug against the fabric.

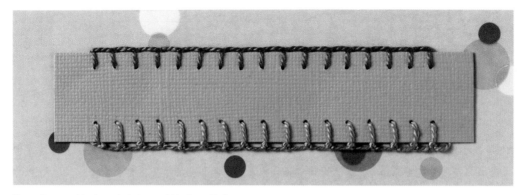

Top to bottom: blanket stitch, knotted blanket stitch

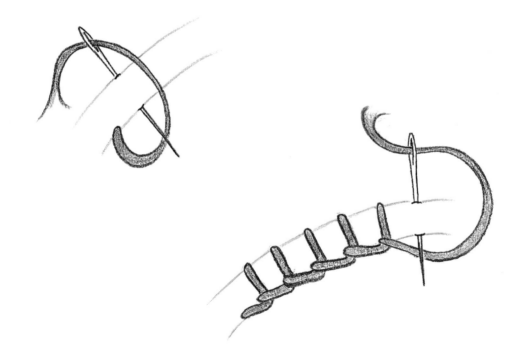

KNOTTED BLANKET STITCH

just like blanket stitch with a tiny knot at each stitch

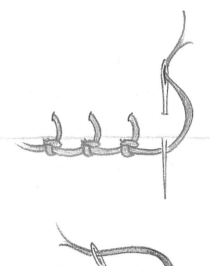

Working from left to right on the edge of the fabric, bring the needle up from the back a bit from the edge and make a blanket stitch. Before moving to the next blanket stitch, loop the needle behind the two threads that hang from the edge of the fabric. To keep even tension, you may find it helpful to hold the top of the blanket stitch while you make the knot. Repeat as you would for the blanket stitch, inserting the needle into the right side of the fabric and taking the next stitch a bit to the right of the previous stitch.

FRENCH KNOTS

create a raised, round dot that looks like a bead

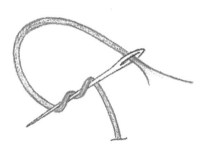

Bring the needle up through to the right side of the fabric. With your free hand, grip the thread about 2" (5 cm) from the spot and pull it taut but not tight. Wind the thread that is between your fingers and the fabric around the needle once. Continue holding the thread taut, while inserting the needle back into the starting point hole (or very close to it). Pull the thread through the wound loop and fabric to the wrong side. Secure the thread after each French knot. For larger knots, wind the thread around the needle two or three times. These are also called bullion stitches.

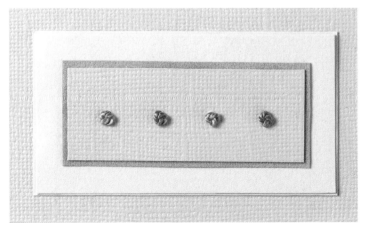

French knots

BACKSTITCH

creates a solid line of end-to-end dashes

Bring the needle up to the right side of the fabric one stitch length from the starting point. Insert the needle at the starting point. Then bring it up again, two stitch lengths away. Pull the thread through, making a stitch. Repeat the first step, inserting your needle at the end of the stitch you just made.

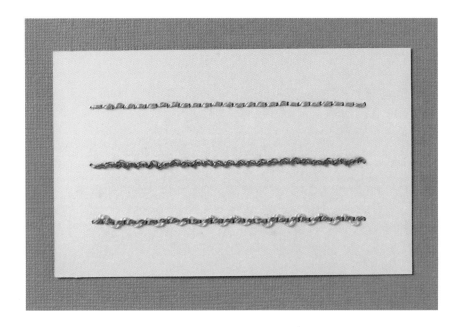

Top to bottom:
backstitch,
whipped backstitch,
woven backstitch

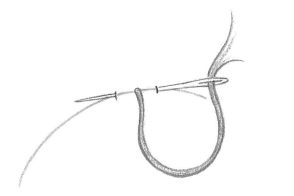
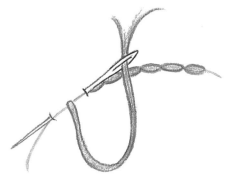

WHIPPED BACKSTITCH

creates a raised, twisted line that looks like a small cord

Make a base line of backstitches. Begin the whipping step at the starting point of the base row. Use a tapestry needle to lace under a backstitch, whip the thread over it, then lace the thread under the following backstitch.

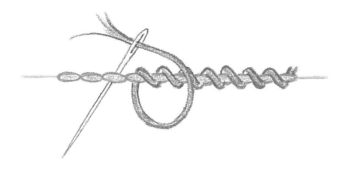

WOVEN BACKSTITCH

an extra thread snakes back and forth under the backstitches

Stitch a base row of backstitches. Use a tapestry needle to weave under a backstitch from the top to the bottom. Then weave under the following stitch from the bottom to the top.

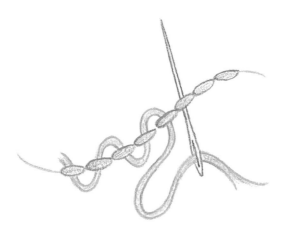

DOUBLE WOVEN BACKSTITCH

two extra threads snake back and forth under the backstitches

Stitch a row of woven backstitches. Start a new thread working the same way as the woven backstitch, filling in the empty spaces on the opposite side.

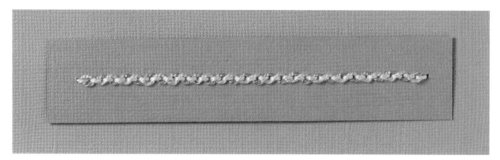

Double woven backstitch

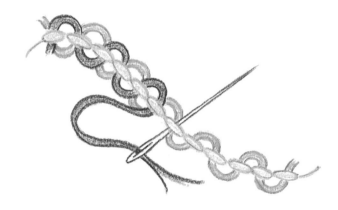

SPLIT STITCH

looks like a small tight chain stitch

Make a small straight stitch. Then bring the needle to the right side again halfway along the stitch you've just made, splitting the thread with the tip of the needle. Repeat to the end of the line.

STEM STITCH

looks like a narrow twisted cord

Bring the needle up on your pattern line and take a small stitch. Come back up close alongside the last stitch, at about the halfway point of the stitch. Take another stitch and come up alongside it. Repeat to the end of the line.

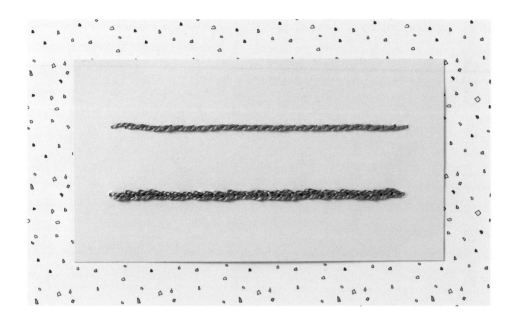

Top to bottom:
split stitch,
stem stitch

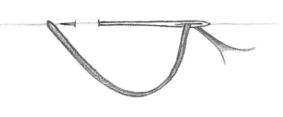
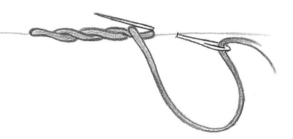

WHIPPED STEM STITCH

looks like a slightly raised cord

Stem stitch a base line. Begin the whipping step at the starting point of the base line. Use a tapestry needle to lace under a stitch, whip the thread over it, then lace the thread under the following stitch.

GET CREATIVE

TIP

Lay a large towel on your workspace to keep beads from scattering.

ADD BEADS

Beads add a little sparkle and dimension to your embroidery. Simply thread up a beading needle with beading thread and stitch beads into your embroidered design. Here's how:

- A single bead can be added by sliding it onto your beading needle down the thread to the fabric. When you insert your needle back into the fabric, the bead will be secured in place. Make a small tight knot on the wrong side of the fabric.

- To secure several single beads spaced apart, secure the first one with a stitch and a knot, as above. Then keep your needle threaded and "carry the thread" on the underside of the fabric to the next location. Again, add a bead, stitch and knot. Continue to carry the thread between beads. When you come to the end of your thread, tie a tight double knot. After you've finished attaching all of the beads, snip the carried threads close to the knots.

- For extra protection, put a tiny dab of fabric glue on every knot on the back of your fabric when you're finished beading.

- To attach beads in a line, string four or five beads onto your thread and insert the needle into the fabric after the last bead. Backstitch, bringing the needle up between the first and second beads. Then pass the needle back through the remaining beads again. Add a few more beads and repeat until you have all of your beads in a row.

- To attach a long strand of beads, string the beads; then position the strand on your project and couch (page 86) the strand down, bringing the needle over the strand where it will settle between beads. Skip a few beads between couching stitches, and continue to the end of the line.

ADD PAINT

Painted designs on fabric items can be enhanced with embroidery. Paints formulated especially for use on fabric stay pliable after repeated laundering. You can also mix acrylic craft paints with a textile medium to make them suitable for fabric painting. Some fabric paint has to be heat-set with an iron and some manufacturers recommend waiting 24 hours before laundering the item. Follow the manufacturer's instructions. Here are some of the ways you can apply paint to fabric:

- Wield a brush and freely hand paint whatever you like. Be brave!

- Use fabric paint or craft paint/textile medium mixture for stenciling, too.

- Apply paint to fabric using rubber stamps. Spread a thin layer of paint on a paper plate and dip the stamp into it, or apply paint to the stamp with a foam brush. Always test first. Be sure to clean your rubber stamps thoroughly before the paint dries.

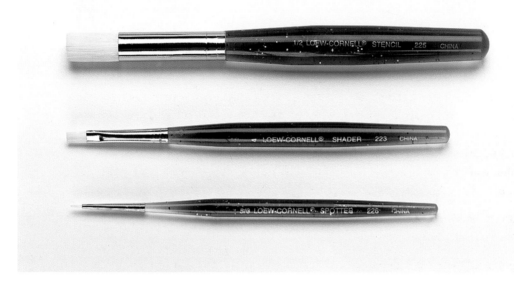

Top to bottom: stencil brush, shader, spotter

STITCH ON PAPER AND CARDSTOCK

Embroidery techniques for fabric can also be used for paper. You can attach vellum and embellishments with stitches. Make a pocket to hold a secret note. Stitch borders and titles and designs. You can stitch letters and words by drawing them freehand or by tracing letter templates or stencils with a disappearing marker. For a finished look, fill the letters in with colored pencil, chalk, or paper paint.

The running stitch and cross-stitch are favorites of paper crafters, but you can do so many more! Play with a variety of embroidery stitches on paper or cardstock before using them on a project. Satin stitch, however, doesn't work well on paper, because the stitches are so close together that the paper tends to tear. You can embroider satin stitches on craft felt and then

TIP

Paper often tears and crumples easily during stitching. Solve that problem by adhering the paper to cardstock with spray adhesive.

attach it to your cardstock with double-sided sticky tape. The one big trick for stitching on paper and cardstock is to prepunch the stitching holes. Here's how:

1. Mark the paper/cardstock with dots where you want the stitches to be.

2. Place a self-healing cutting mat on your work surface. On top of that, put your mouse pad, facedown.

3. Put the cardstock on the mouse pad and use a piercer, such as an awl, stiletto, or large chenille needle, to poke holes where you want to stitch.

4. Use a tapestry needle to lace your thread through the holes.

5. Secure the thread on the back of the paper with tape rather than a knot.

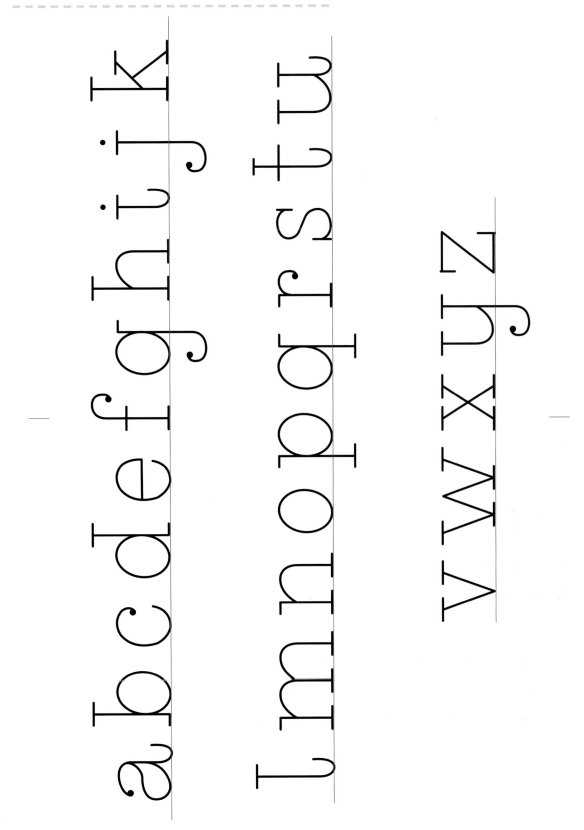

TYPEWRITER TYPE-OGRAPHY

a b c d e f g h i

j k l m n o p q r

s t u v w x y z

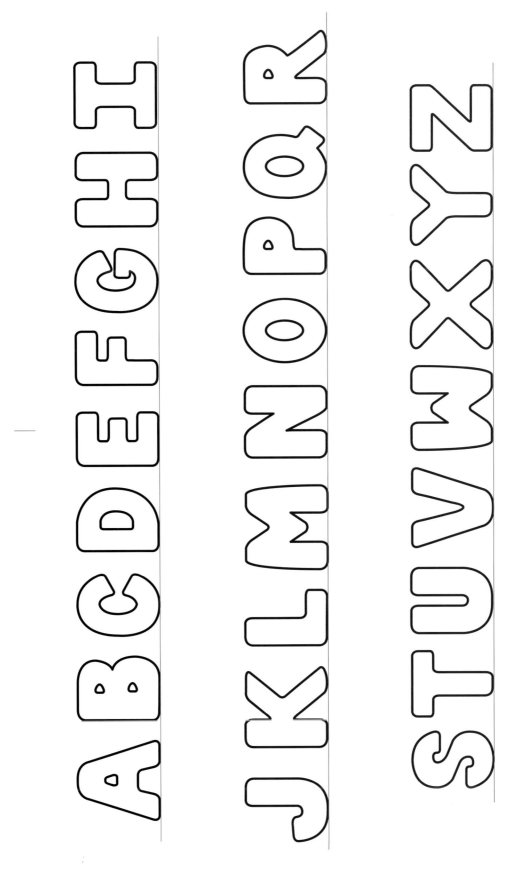

BUBBLE GRAFFITI A–Zs

ELEGANT CLASSIC CALLIGRAPHY (upper case)

ELEGANT CLASSIC CALLIGRAPHY (lower case)

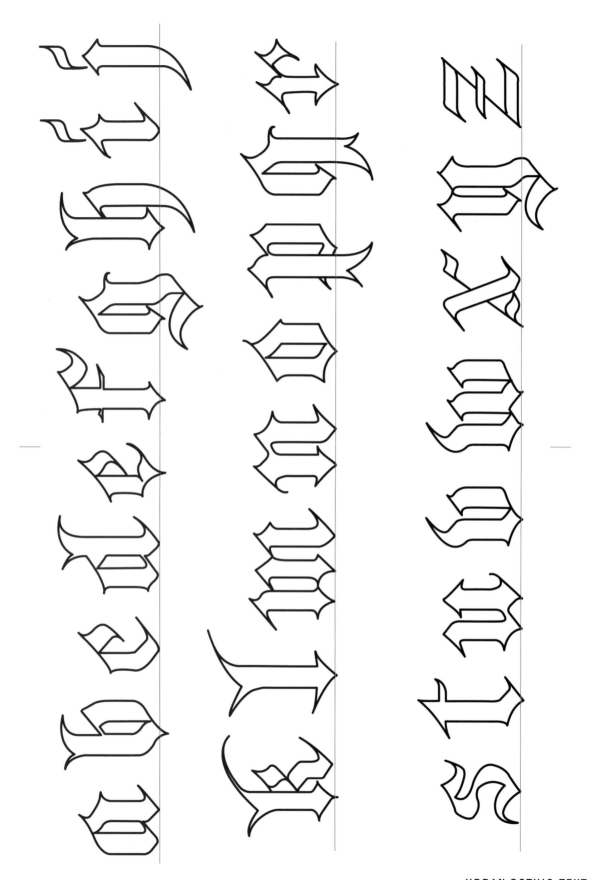

URBAN GOTHIC TEXT

Sources

The following products were used for the projects:

THINKING CAP
DMC Pearl Cotton: very dark royal blue 820
Craft Cap: Article #7170871 by An Accessory Network, www.accessorynetwork.com

BRAVO LABEL
DMC Pearl Cotton: very dark blue violet 333

BASEBALL TEE
DMC Pearl Cotton: red 321, medium tangerine 741, and lemon 307

LOVE CARD
DMC Pearl Cotton: lemon 307 and plum 718
DMC Cotton Embroidery Floss: plum 718
Cardstock: tangerine, thin striped, and solid pumpkin from Lasting Impressions for Paper, Inc., www.lastingimpressions.com
Dot paper, light and medium grape from Frances Meyer, Inc. #5006-863, www.francesmeyer.com

SWEET DREAMS LULLABY LINENS
Au Ver A Soie Silk Embroidery Floss: overdyed silk thread, waterlillies
DMC Cotton Embroidery Floss: ecru, ultra very light shell pink 225
Mill Hill: ultraluscent seed beads, rose petite beads, 62024
Mill Hill: Glass Treasures, clear star 12061

PERSONALIZED PILLOWCASE
DMC Pearl Cotton: light lemon 445, cranberry 603
Pillowcase: Isaac Mizrahi, Target
Offray: red grosgrain ribbon, 3/8" (9 mm)

SPIT HAPPENS BURP CLOTH
DMC Pearl Cotton: Delft blue 809
DMC Cotton Embroidery Floss: Color Variations green/blue 4020, yellow/green

ALOHA TEE
DMC Pearl Cotton: cranberry 603, light cranberry 604

XOX TEE
DMC Cotton Embroidery Floss: light wedgewood 519
Pellon Easy Knit fusible knit interfacing

ROCK ME JEAN JACKET
DMC Light Effects Precious Metals Floss: copper E301
Krylon: copper leafing pen

SUPER INITIAL JEANS
DMC Pearl Cotton: light turquoise 598, plum 718, very dark blue violet 333
Felted wool: JoAnn Fabrics, 1930's Assortment, 8011330

MONOGRAM CUFF
DMC Cotton Embroidery Floss: white blanc

I DO! KEEPSAKE RIBBON
Au Ver A Soie Silk Embroidery Floss: medium rose 4634, www.auverasoie.com
Therm O Web, Heat'nBond Iron-on Adhesive Hem

CREWEL MONOGRAM PILLOW
DMC Medicis Crewel Wool: 100% wool tapestry yarn, green 8414
DMC Pearl Cotton: black 310
DMC Cotton Embroidery Floss: black 310

BLING TEE
DMC Metallic Thread: light silver 283ZA
Mill Hill: silver beads

MOM CHRISTMAS STOCKING
DMC Medicis Crewel Wool: 100% wool tapestry yarn, sugar plum 8896

GIRLS TEE
DMC Pearl Cotton: light parrot green 907, raspberry sherbet 3806, white blanc
DMC Cottom Embroidery Floss: raspberry sherbet 3806

TICKLED PINK ONESIE
Onesie: just one year, a division of Carter's style, #510-073
Fuzzy Pink Yarn: Yarn Bee, Playful, Ice Princess Solid #08 www.hobbylobby.com
DMC Light Effects Floss: pearlescent E5200

SAY CHEESE CAMERA TAG
DMC Cotton Embroidery Floss: light parrot green 907 and black 310
Luggage Tag: Creating Keepsakes, PRIMEDIA #BETOS 001B www.creatingkeepsakes.com
Offray: black and white ribbon, 1/4" (7 mm)
Star charm: Simply Beading, #0705, NOTEWORTHY, Chatsworth, CA 91311

SMILE TAG
DMC Cotton Embroidery Floss: light parrot green 907
DMC Pearl Cotton: bright orange red 606

Acknowledgements

Many thanks to DMC Corporation, Fiskars Brands, Inc., and Lowe-Cornell, Inc. for providing materials for this book.

Our unending gratitude and love to Jim Jankowicz for the moral and all other types of support that he continually and generously lavishes on us. We love you more!

Thanks to our mentors Belva Gadladge and Kelly Hoernig. We couldn't have started or finished this book without your kind, priceless guidance and encouragement.

To Alison Brown Cerier and Linda Neubauer at CPi, we sincerely appreciate your formidable insight, direction, and patience!

Dedication

We dedicate this book to all of the wonderful, nurturing people who have passed on a legacy of love and needlework knowledge to a new generation, especially our own Grandma Barbara Harrison, Grandma Amy Morris, Gram/Mom Ree Morris, Great Aunt Angeline Brunke, and Great Grandma "Nanny" Angeline Kondal who was still crocheting gifts at age 102! Bless your hearts!

In memory of our creative muse Susan Smith, Decatur Area Arts Council Executive Director, and Kristin's art angel, MacArthur High School art teacher, Mr. Spangler.